The Easy Will and Living Will Kit

(+ CD-ROM)

Joy S. Chambers
Attorney at Law

SPHINX® PUBLISHING
AN IMPRINT OF SOURCEBOOKS, INC.®
NAPERVILLE, ILLINOIS
www.SphinxLegal.com

First Edition: 2005
Second Printing: November, 2005

Published by: Sphinx® Publishing, An Imprint of Sourcebooks, Inc.®

Naperville Office
P.O. Box 4410
Naperville, Illinois 60567-4410
630-961-3900
Fax: 630-961-2168
www.sourcebooks.com
www.SphinxLegal.com

This publication is designed to provide accurate and authoritative information in regard to the subject matter covered. It is sold with the understanding that the publisher is not engaged in rendering legal, accounting, or other professional service. If legal advice or other expert assistance is required, the services of a competent professional person should be sought.

From a Declaration of Principles Jointly Adopted by a Committee of the American Bar Association and a Committee of Publishers and Associations

This product is not a substitute for legal advice.

Disclaimer required by Texas statutes.

The author is not engaged in the rendering of professional services in this book. The author specifically disclaims any responsibility for any liability loss or risk, personal or otherwise, which is incurred as a consequence, direct or indirect, of the use or application of any of the contents of this book.

Library of Congress Cataloging-in-Publication Data
Chambers, Joy, attorney at law.
  The easy will and living will kit (with CD-ROM) / by Joy
Chambers.-- 1st ed.
    p. cm.
  Includes index.
  ISBN 1-57248-481-0 (pbk. : alk. paper)
  1. Wills--United States--Popular works. 2. Right to die--Law and legislation--United States--Popular works. 3. Power of attorney--United States--Popular works. I. Title.

KF755.Z9C435 2005
346.7305'4--dc22
                                                              2005015523

Printed and bound in the United States of America.
BG — 10 9 8 7 6 5 4 3 2

This book is dedicated to Edna and Charles Hilsenroth, exemplars of successful aging, and unfailingly supportive over the decades.

Acknowledgment

Writing is considered a solitary task, but no one produces a book alone. I would like to express my deepest gratitude to Joy Davis, whose creativity, ingenuity, and professionalism are unparalleled. My warmest appreciation to my team at Sourcebooks—editor Michael Bowen and publicist Allison Thomas. A sincere thank you to Allan Lefcowitz and Jane Fox, who supported me at the outset; Jeff Kleinman, who remains my unflappable agent; and my office team, Viola Miller and Barbara Peters, who are as unfazed by publishing deadlines as they are by the other demands of a hectic law practice. My appreciation as well to the attorneys who encouraged me and vetted the legal tools in this book: Ira Lowe, Sally Determan, Charles Sabatino, and David English.

Contents

Chapter 3: The Self-Proving Affidavit 73

How to Use the CD-ROM

Thank you for purchasing *The Easy Will and Living Will Kit*. We have worked hard to provide you with all of the essential documents you need to have your estate and personal well-being in order. To make this material even more useful, we have included every document found in the Appendix on a CD-ROM that is attached to the inside back cover of the book.

Use the list on the CD-ROM for help finding the form you are looking for. You can use these forms just as you would the forms in the book. Print them out, fill them in, and use them however you need. You can also fill in the forms directly on your computer. Just identify the form you need, open it, click on the space where the information should go, and input your information. Customize each form for your particular needs. Use them over and over again.

The CD-ROM is compatible with both PC and Mac operating systems. (While it should work with either operating system, we cannot guarantee that it will work with your particular system and we cannot provide technical assistance.) To use the forms on your computer, you will need to use Adobe Reader. (Previous versions of this program were called Acrobat Reader.) The CD-ROM does not contain this program. You can download this program from Adobe's website at **www.adobe.com**. Click on the "Get Adobe Reader" icon to begin the download process and follow the instructions.

Once you have the program installed, insert the CD-ROM into your computer. Double click on the icon representing the disc on your desktop or go through your hard drive to identify the drive that contains the disc and click on it.

Once opened, you will see the files contained on the CD-ROM listed as "Form #: [Form Title]." Open the file you need through Adobe Reader. You may print the form to fill it out manually at this point, or your can use the "Hand Tool" and click on the appropriate line to fill it in using your computer.

Any time you see bracketed information [ ] on the form, you can click on it and delete the bracketed information from your final form. This information is only a reference guide to assist you in filling in the forms and should be removed from your final version. Once all your information is filled in, you can print your filled-in form.

NOTE: *Adobe Reader does not allow you to save the PDF with the boxes filled in.*

. . . .

Purchasers of this book are granted a license to use the forms contained in it for their own personal use. By purchasing this book, you have also purchased a limited license to use all forms on the accompanying CD-ROM. The license limits you to personal use only and all other copyright laws must be adhered. No claim of copyright is made in any government form reproduced in the book or on the CD-ROM. You are free to modify the forms and tailor them to your specific situation.

The author and publisher have attempted to provide the most current and up-to-date information available. However, the courts, Congress, and your state's legislatures review, modify, and change laws on an ongoing basis, as well as create new laws from time to time. By the very nature of the information and due to the continual changes in our legal system, to be sure that you have the current and best information for your situation, you should consult a local attorney or research the current laws yourself.

. . . .

This publication is designed to provide accurate and authoritative information in regard to the subject matter covered. It is sold with the understanding that the publisher is not engaged in rendering legal, accounting, or other professional service. If legal advice or other expert assistance is required, the services of a competent professional person should be sought.

> —*From a Declaration of Principles Jointly Adopted by a Committee of the American Bar Association and a Committee of Publishers and Associations*

This product is not a substitute for legal advice.

> —*Disclaimer required by Texas statutes.*

Using Self-Help Law Books

Before using a self-help law book, you should realize the advantages and disadvantages of doing your own legal work and understand the challenges and diligence that this requires.

The Growing Trend

Rest assured that you won't be the first or only person handling your own legal matter. For example, in some states, more than seventy-five percent of the people in divorces and other cases represent themselves. Because of the high cost of legal services, this is a major trend and many courts are struggling to make it easier for people to represent themselves. However, some courts are not happy with people who do not use attorneys and refuse to help them in any way. For some, the attitude is, "Go to the law library and figure it out for yourself."

We write and publish self-help law books to give people an alternative to the often complicated and confusing legal books found in most law libraries. We have made the explanations of the law as simple and easy to understand as possible. Of course, unlike an attorney advising an individual client, we cannot cover every conceivable possibility.

Cost/Value Analysis

Whenever you shop for a product or service, you are faced with various levels of quality and price. In deciding what product or service to buy, you make a cost/value analysis on the basis of your willingness to pay and the quality you desire.

When buying a car, you decide whether you want transportation, comfort, status, or sex appeal. Accordingly, you decide among such choices as a Neon, a Lincoln, a Rolls Royce, or a Porsche. Before making a decision, you usually weigh the merits of each option against the cost.

When you get a headache, you can take a pain reliever (such as aspirin) or visit a medical specialist for a neurological examination. Given this choice, most people, of course, take a pain reliever, since it costs only pennies; whereas a medical examination costs hundreds of dollars and takes a lot of time. This is usually a logical choice because it is rare to need anything more than a pain reliever for a headache. But in some cases, a headache may indicate a brain tumor and failing to see a specialist right away can result in complications. Should everyone with a headache go to a specialist? Of course not, but people treating their own illnesses must realize that they are betting on the basis of their cost/value analysis of the situation. They are taking the most logical option.

The same cost/value analysis must be made when deciding to do one's own legal work. Many legal situations are very straight forward, requiring a simple form and no complicated analysis. Anyone with a little intelligence and a book of instructions can handle the matter without outside help.

But there is always the chance that complications are involved that only an attorney would notice. To simplify the law into a book like this, several legal cases often must be condensed into a single sentence or paragraph. Otherwise, the book would be several hundred pages long and too complicated for most people. However, this simplification necessarily leaves out many details and nuances that would apply to special or unusual situations. Also, there are many ways to interpret most legal questions. Your case may come before a judge who disagrees with the analysis of our authors.

Therefore, in deciding to use a self-help law book and to do your own legal work, you must realize that you are making a cost/value analysis. You have decided that the money you will save in doing it yourself outweighs the chance that your case will not turn out to your satisfaction. Most people handling their own simple legal matters never have a problem, but occasionally people find that it ended up costing them more to have an attorney straighten out the situation than it would have if they had hired an attorney in the beginning. Keep this in mind while handling your case, and be sure to consult an attorney if you feel you might need further guidance.

Local Rules

The next thing to remember is that a book which covers the law for the entire nation, or even for an entire state, cannot possibly include every procedural difference of every jurisdiction. Whenever possible, we provide the exact form needed; however, in some areas, each county, or even each judge, may require unique forms and procedures. In our state books, our forms usually cover the majority of counties in the state, or provide examples of the type of form which will be required. In our national books, our forms are sometimes even more general in nature but are designed to give a good idea of the type of form that will be needed in most locations. Nonetheless, keep in mind that your state, county, or judge may have a requirement, or use a form, that is not included in this book.

You should not necessarily expect to be able to get all of the information and resources you need solely from within the pages of this book. This book will serve as your guide, giving you specific information whenever possible and helping you to find out what else you will need to know. This is just like if you decided to build your own backyard deck. You might purchase a book on how to build decks. However, such a book would not include the building codes and permit requirements of every city, town, county, and township in the nation; nor would it include the lumber, nails, saws, hammers, and other materials and tools you would need to actually build the deck. You would use the book as your guide, and then do some work and research involving such matters as whether you need a permit of some kind, what type and grade of wood are available in your area, whether to use hand tools or power tools, and how to use those tools.

Changes in the Law

Before using the forms in a book like this, you should check with your court clerk to see if there are any local rules of which you should be aware, or local forms you will need to use. Often, such forms will require the same information as the forms in the book but are merely laid out differently or use slightly different language. They will sometimes require additional information.

Besides being subject to local rules and practices, the law is subject to change at any time. The courts and the legislatures of all fifty states are constantly revising the laws. It is possible that while you are reading this book, some aspect of the law is being changed.

In most cases, the change will be of minimal significance. A form will be redesigned, additional information will be required, or a waiting period will be extended. As a result, you might need to revise a form, file an extra form, or wait out a longer time period; these types of changes will not usually affect the outcome of your case. On the other hand, sometimes a major part of the law is changed, the entire law in a particular area is rewritten, or a case that was the basis of a central legal point is overruled. In such instances, your entire ability to pursue your case may be impaired.

Again, you should weigh the value of your case against the cost of an attorney and make a decision as to what you believe is in your best interest.

Introduction

Americans are independent spirits. We do not like being told how to manage any aspect of our lives. And yet, many of us have never taken the necessary legal steps to ensure that our wishes are respected when critical decisions must be made. Have you thought about what would happen about if you had a fatal auto accident—would your property be distributed as you wished? If you survived the accident but had a long recuperation, who will see that your bills get paid? And, if you took a turn for the worse, who would be in the position of making life-or-death decisions about your treatment?

This book was written to help you through the steps necessary to safeguard your future, as well as the futures of your loved ones. It contains the basic information and forms you need to make a valid Will, designate someone to manage your financial affairs if you are ever incapacitated, and appoint someone to ensure your stated wishes are followed if you become critically or terminally ill. *Putting your affairs in order* need not be nerve-racking, time-consuming, or expensive. While the phrase may have an ominous ring, it is actually one of the most life-affirming things you will ever do.

Many people assume that, in the absence of an up-to-date Will and designated agents for finances and medical care, someone close to them can be trusted to make the right decisions. That may be true, but why risk it when so much is at stake? And why add stress to loved ones who want to carry out your wishes, but are not sure what they are? In the most loving of families, there can be honest differences of opinion. Once you have attended to these matters, you will be relieved and pleased that you have met your legal obligations to yourself and your loved ones.

How This Book Can Help You

I was inspired to write this book when, having written thousands of Wills for others over the years, I saw how the process could be simplified for the vast majority of Americans. Nearly all of my clients fit into one of six *life situations*, depending on their marital status, children, and stage of life. Those six life situations are:

1. unmarried;
2. married without children;
3. married with young children;
4. married with adult children;
5. widowed, divorced, or unmarried with young children; and,
6. widowed, divorced, or unmarried with adult children.

To simplify the process of making a Will, this book includes six Will forms—one for each situation—with detailed instructions on how to complete them.

Although people are individuals, their everyday lives are usually similar. They have some property—bank accounts, real estate, automobiles, jewelry, and so on. Most do not have multimillion dollar businesses, complex tax issues, or huge debt. They usually just want their money to pass—as easily as possible—to their family members. They also want to make sure that if or when they cannot act for themselves, someone they trust is in a position to act for them.

Most people express similar wishes when they make a Will. If they are married, they want their spouse to inherit their property. If their spouse is deceased, they want their children (or grandchildren, if a child is deceased) to inherit their property in equal shares. Without a spouse or children, people usually wish to leave their property to a combination of relatives and close friends. The forms take these facts into account, further simplifying the Will-making process.

As an attorney, I understand that legal documents can be intimidating. While a Will does have the force of a complex legal system behind it, writing it can be fairly simple. Lawyers have been writing Wills—and courts have been interpreting them—for centuries. Since the law has developed standard language that meets the needs of most people, they can save money and time by using a form designed for their life situation that incorporates the most popular options for leaving the property they own to others.

You can benefit from what my clients have taught me. The Will forms in this book are designed to meet the needs of most people, while satisfying the legal requirements for a Will to be valid. The accompanying instructions go into as much detail as you need—and no more! In addition to the six simple Will forms, I have included a form called a *Self-Proving Affidavit,* with instructions for completing and attaching to your new Will. This simple form, in which a notary public attests that your Will has been properly signed and witnessed, can simplify the process of probating your Will and distributing your property.

Also included are forms and instructions for a *Financial Power of Attorney* and an *Advance Directive for Health Care.* The latter incorporates the provisions of a *Living Will* and a *Health Care Power of Attorney* into a single document.

A word for those who find that a simple Will will not suffice—the information in this book can help make you a more knowledgeable client, so you are still likely to save money and time when you seek an attorney's advice.

Getting the Most from This Book

The contents of this book are organized to correspond to the three legal documents necessary to put your affairs in order—a simple Will, a Financial Power of Attorney, and a Health Care Advance Directive. I highly recommend that you complete all three to fully protect your loved ones and yourself.

First, you need to have a basic understanding of what each document can and cannot do; how each is activated and its provisions enforced; and, the varied roles individuals play in each. Be sure to review the information provided in the front of each major section before proceeding to the forms and instructions. Additional information is incorporated into "A Conversation About…" sections which conveys key points in a lively lawyer-to-client format. Examples that relate to each form, sample completed forms, and answers to frequently asked questions are also included.

The forms contained in this book to help you to prepare a Power of Attorney for Finances and a Health Care Advance Directive are intended for general use. Unlike the Will forms, virtually everyone can use these forms to plan for the future. Please note, however, that these are important legal documents. Be careful to follow all instructions on completing and storing them. Finally, if you have questions that have not been addressed in the text, err on the side of caution and see a lawyer.

When Not to Use This Book

This book is intended to guide you through the process of planning for the future in a simple, straightforward manner. Nine out of ten people share similar life situations and express similar wishes about their plans for the future. There are, however, exceptions. You may have special family or financial circumstances, where having a lawyer prepare your Will is necessary. Consider the following circumstances. If one describes you, see a lawyer for a Will tailored especially for your needs.

- ◆ Your spouse is living at the time of your death and you do not want him or her to inherit *all* of your property. If you wish to leave some of your property to anyone else—including your parents or any and all children—you should not use any of the Will forms in this book.

- ◆ Your spouse is living at the time of your death and he or she cannot manage finances very well. You need to consider leaving property to your spouse in a trust. For that, you need legal advice.

- ◆ You do not want your children to inherit your property in equal shares, in the event that your spouse predeceases you. (This includes your desire to disinherit a child.) The forms in this book were not designed to cover this situation.

- ◆ Your spouse predeceases you and you are concerned about a child inheriting money because he or she cannot manage money, needs special care, or otherwise needs a trust.

- ◆ You have children from a prior marriage and your intention is that they inherit the remainder of your estate, should your spouse die after inheriting your property as primary beneficiary. You need to consider leaving property to your spouse in a trust, which requires legal advice.

- ◆ You have neither a spouse nor children and you want your property to go to a charity or an unusual combination of people and organizations.

If your own situation does not clearly fit into one of the six scenarios described in this book, do not try to make one work. Instead, see a lawyer to make sure that your Will is a perfect fit. It may cost less in the long run. If any of the following situations apply in your life, do not use the Will forms in this book.

- ◆ You have accumulated a large estate and need to consult a lawyer to minimize inheritance taxes. Currently, federal estate taxes are limited to estates totaling more than $1.5 million (including home equity and real estate).

- ◆ You have entered into a prenuptial agreement, which a lawyer will need to review to assure that your Will conforms to the agreement.

◆ You have made large gifts in your lifetime, which may complicate your estate tax situation.

Louisiana

Do not use the Will forms in this book if you live in Louisiana, where the state laws are based on the Napoleonic Code.

Contested Situations

If you have any indication that anyone might contest your Will, see a lawyer. Grounds for contesting a Will are the writer's mental incompetence, or that it was executed fraudulently or under duress. In addition, you cannot make a Will that violates your state's laws of inheritance. For instance, your spouse is entitled to a specified share of your estate.

The vast majority of Wills are not contested and even fewer are overturned. Still, if you have concerns, talk them over with a lawyer.

It is my hope that you will live a richly rewarding life and that, having put your legal affairs in order, you will enjoy increased peace of mind about the future.

Frequently Asked Questions

Wills

Q: How old do you have to be to make a Will?

A: In most states, you need to be at least 18 years of age and of sound mind. Some states allow younger people to make a Will if they are married, in the military, or legally emancipated (which confers adult status).

Q: Do I need to make a new Will if I move to another state?

A: Nearly all states accept Wills written in other states. The forms in this book will work in all states except Louisiana, which has unique requirements because its state law is based on the *Napoleonic Code*.

Q: Can I revoke my Will whenever I wish?

A: Yes. In all the Will forms in this book, there is a clause revoking earlier Wills. You may also revoke them by simply destroying them. However, you do need an updated Will. (See Chapter 7 for more information about changing your Will.)

Q: Can I have more than one executor or trustee?

A: Yes, but it is generally not a good idea. Each has to consent to every action and each needs to sign all documents. Obviously, it is easier to obtain one signature than two on the myriad of court documents required when going through probate or administering a trust.

Q: What are the most important qualities in selecting an executor or trustee?

A: First and foremost, you must have absolute trust in this person to carry out your wishes responsibly and professionally. Second, he or she should be in good health and able to do the work required. The executor or trustee needs to get along well with your beneficiaries, and of course, be willing to serve. A resident of your state is preferable, though not essential.

Q: How can I make sure my pets are cared for after I am gone?

A: Although many consider their pets to be part of the family, pets cannot inherit money or property in a Will. You can, however, use your Will to provide for a good home and care for them. The easiest way is to leave your pet to someone you trust, and leave them money for care. Some states allow trusts to be established for a pet, but this can be a costly and complicated procedure.

Q: I have minor children and their mother is deceased. Can you give me guidance in selecting an appropriate guardian?

A: People usually choose a family member, such as an aunt or uncle, who is fairly close to them. Age, health, and marital status are considerations, especially since you would not want your children being uprooted again. Child-rearing skills and lifestyles are also important in making a decision.

Q: Do I put my wishes for burial or cremation in my Will?

A: No. Decisions about funerals or cremations must be made days before the Will is located and read. Your Will cannot be used to legally enforce these wishes. Write out what you want to happen and give the instructions to a family member.

Q: Do I put my wishes for organ donations in my Will?

A: No. By the time your Will is located and read, it is too late to make these donations. As part of your comprehensive planning for the future, complete the *Health Care Advance Directive* in Chapter 4, which incorporates your wishes regarding organ donation into a Living Will.

Q: I have accumulated a lot of debts recently. If I die, will that affect my wishes for leaving property to my children?

A: One of the main duties of your executor is to pay all legitimate debts. An effort will be made to assure that all are accounted for before your property is distributed. If you leave property to people but do not have enough other assets to pay your debts, the property you designated will instead be sold to pay the debts. If your total debt is larger than your total estate, nothing will be left for your heirs—but, at least, they will not inherit you debts.

Q: Maybe this is silly, but I have a feeling that if I make a Will, I will die soon after. Am I the only person who feels this way?

A: You are not alone in being superstitious about making a Will. Others put it off because they have fallen prey to the mystique of making a Will. They think it has to be complicated and expensive, and that they need a lawyer. For most Americans, that simply is not true. (And by the time you have needed to update your Will several times, you will be laughing about your superstition.)

Advance Health Care Directive (Living Will)

Q: Am I giving up control over my care by naming an agent?

A: Not at all. Physicians and health care facilities are legally bound to discuss treatment options with you as long as you have the capacity to make decisions and the ability to communicate them. When you are unconscious, irrational, or unable to make an informed decision, your agent is required to make decisions that are in your best interest. In fact, you have *more* control over your care, because you have someone speaking for you when you cannot speak for yourself.

Q: Who should have a Health Care Advance Directive?

A: Everyone should arrange to have their wishes known regarding medical treatment in critical or terminal circumstances as soon as they become legal adults—18 years of age in most states. While specifying the type and extent of treatment traditionally has been considered a concern of the elderly and infirmed, consider this: young, physically vital people may face a longer time on life support—perhaps decades—if they are critically injured.

Q: How often should I change my advance directive?

A: Change your advance directive when you change your mind about its provisions or your choice of an agent. Presumably, you have given both careful consideration, so you should not need to update your directive very often.

Q: Are Health Care Advance Directives legally valid in all states?

A: Yes. All states have laws permitting individuals to sign documents expressing their wishes about health care decisions when they cannot speak for themselves. Although the specific laws differ, the underlying principle of respecting a patient's wishes is contained in all of them. The laws give great weight to any form of written directive.

Q: There are many health care forms available. How can I choose the best one?

A: The form in this book was recently created by the American Bar Association, and is the best currently available. It incorporates the provisions of a Living Will with a Power of Attorney for Health Care, so you have only one comprehensive form to complete. It also gives you the most leeway to express your particular wishes reflecting your values and priorities. That said, many states have created state-specific forms that can be found on the Internet. The *National Hospice and Palliative Care Organization* sponsors a website, **www.caringinfo.org**, that provides state forms and other useful information.

Q: Can I name my physician as my agent? It seems like a simple solution.

A: Some states put limits on who you can name. These include your physician, staff members at your health care institution, the agent you have named in your Financial Power of Attorney, employees of any government agencies financially responsible for your care, and anyone serving as an agent for ten or more people. Most people name their spouse or a responsible adult child as their agent.

Q: I would like to help someone else live by donating my major organs for transplantation. The custom in our family is to have a viewing and an open-casket funeral. Is that possible?

A: Yes. Your family could observe its usual mourning customs, with the additional consolation that you brought joy and hope to other families with critically ill loved ones.

Power of Attorney

Q: Can I still manage my own affairs after creating a Financial Power of Attorney?

A: Absolutely. All you are doing is assuring that you will have an agent when you need one. Your Power of Attorney becomes effective as soon as you sign it, but your agent needs the original signed, notarized form before he or she can act on your behalf. So, even though you have authorized your agent to manage your money, you have retained the power by keeping the original form in your possession.

Q: With so many Power of Attorney forms available, how can I be sure to choose the best one?

A: The form provided in this book is derived from the uniform model law drafted by the *National Conference on Uniform State Laws*, and represents a step forward in simplifying the process. This form makes it easy to designate which transactions you want your agent to perform.

Q: What is a General Power of Attorney?

A: A General Power of Attorney authorizes your agent to manage any and all of your finances. In the example on page 114, John gave Mary a General Power of Attorney. Using the form in this book, you create a General Power of Attorney by initialing the line before the letter "N" on the first page of the form.

Q: What is a Limited Power of Attorney?

A: This is a Power of Attorney that only authorizes your agent to manage specific financial matters. If John wanted Mary to manage his bank accounts, but not his real estate or other financial affairs, he would initial the line in front of line "E" on the form ("banking and other transactions").

Q: What is a Durable Power of Attorney?

A: This is a Power of Attorney that endures, or is still valid, while you are incapacitated. The form in this book creates a Durable Power of Attorney with the following statement.

This Power of Attorney will continue to be effective even though I become disabled, incapacitated, or incompetent.

Q: What happens to my Financial Power of Attorney when I die?

A: Your agent's authority to manage your financial affairs ends upon your death. At that point, your executor will go to court and begin the process of probating your Will.

Q: Can my agent manage my health care?

A: No. You need to create a Power of Attorney for Health Care, which is incorporated into the Health Care Advance Directive included in Chapter 4. You can, however, name the same person as agent on both forms.

Q: What if my agent dies?

A: Immediately execute another Power of Attorney to designate a new agent.

NOTE: *In this form, you do not name any alternates.*

Q: What if I want to revoke the Power of Attorney?

A: If the document has never left your possession, it is easy to revoke. Just tear it up. If you gave a copy of it to your bank, you need to notify your bank *in writing* that you wish to revoke it. How you give notice has to conform to state law. In fact, if your agent has been using your Power of Attorney and you want to revoke it, you may want to consult a lawyer to ensure that you have taken all the necessary steps for revocation.

Q: What do I do if there is no one I trust to act as a financial agent for me?

A: You need to see a lawyer to design a customized Power of Attorney, with additional safeguards in it. You should also consider hiring a professional to act as your agent under a Power of Attorney. Your bank may have a trust department that can help you sort out this problem.

Q: Why do I need to give my spouse a Power of Attorney when we own property jointly?

A: You may not own everything jointly at the time you become incapacitated. Being married does not automatically give your spouse access to all your finances.

Q: Is it a good idea to have multiple agents to police each other's decisions?

A: No. You should not do it for the same reasons that you should not have multiple executors in your Will. It complicates decision-making and increases the opportunities for disagreements that might have to be resolved by a judge in court.

Q: I have been named an agent by someone else, an elderly aunt. How do I sign checks as her financial agent?

A: If you aunt's name is Jane Smith and your name is John Smith, then sign as follows: Jane Smith by her agent, John Smith.

Chapter 1:
What You Need to Know about Wills

The first thing you should know about Wills is that every adult should have one. A carefully considered, up-to-date, legally valid Will that accurately reflects your wishes gives you a greater sense of control over your life.

Before you proceed to the forms in the Chapter 2 (where you will choose the appropriate Will form for your situation), please review the following basic information, which relates to *all* situations.

What is a Will?

Basically, a *Will* is a legal document that provides for the disposition of your property after your death. In it, you name an *executor* to see that your wishes are carried out, under the guidance of the court. You also designate *beneficiaries*, the people to whom you wish to leave your *property*. While you may think of property as real estate, the term encompasses all your possessions—bank accounts, investments, home, car, recreational equipment and vehicles, books, jewelry, and more. The sum of your property and your money is considered your *estate*.

No Will

If you die *intestate* (without a Will), your wishes may not be honored. In fact, they may not be known or understood. Nearly everyone has heard of at least one instance in which the absence of a Will caused great distress among family members. This may not be due to greed, but to varying interpretations of what you would want, sincerely put forth by your loved ones. Among people in the throes of grief, small differences can rapidly escalate into major rifts.

If you die without a Will, a judge will appoint an *administrator* (rather than an executor you would choose) and your property will be distributed according to your state's laws of *intestate succession*. The process may cost considerable money and time, not to mention the emotional havoc wreaked on your survivors. You may have shared your intentions with your loved ones, but only a valid Will can assure that those intentions become reality in *probate court*. (See the next section for a discussion on probate.) Finally, if you die without any relatives that can be located, your estate will go to the state.

Your Will and Probate

On the other hand, if you have a valid Will (*testate*), the person you have named as executor will be responsible for settling your affairs and distributing your property to the *beneficiaries* you have named. You can be assured that your wishes are honored without more stress and strain on your loved ones.

Your property, however, will not automatically pass to your beneficiaries at your death. First, your Will must be *probated*, a legal procedure that takes time. Upon your death, the person you have named your *executor* is responsible for going to court to begin the probate process. The court verifies that your Will is valid, including verification of *witnesses* to the signing of your Will. (This verification can be simplified by the attachment of a Self-Proving Affidavit to your Will as discussed in Chapter 3.) Once your Will is *proven* to be valid, the court-supervised process of transferring your property to your beneficiaries begins.

Your choice of an *executor* is critical. This should be someone you trust implicitly to carry out the provisions of your Will in a professional manner. Many people name a spouse or adult child. It is perfectly legal for someone who will benefit from your Will to serve as executor. In fact, someone with a financial interest may be especially conscientious. In any case, an executor performs his or her duties under the supervision of the court.

Before naming an executor, be sure to discuss it with the person you are considering, as it is a serious commitment. If no one comes immediately to mind, think carefully about any relatives or close friends that you consider reliable. A bank or trust company is a possibility, but modest estates may not be a priority for them and the fees may be considerable.

Some states restrict the right of a nonresident to serve as an executor. It may be permissible by preparing additional paperwork or posting bond, but nevertheless, it should be a consideration.

Probate can be a lengthy, complex process, but you can expedite it by completing a simple document—a Self-Proving Affidavit—and attaching it to your Will. In this form, a notary attests to your witnesses' signatures. As this is an important step in validating your Will, much time can be saved by not having to locate witnesses to testify in court, perhaps years after witnessing your Will.

Limitations of a Will

Some assets—such as retirement plans, life insurance, and other property with named beneficiaries—are not controlled by your Will. They have beneficiary designation clauses, in which the beneficiary named in the account or policy receives the asset rather than the beneficiary named in your Will.

Other assets not controlled by your Will are a pay-on-death bank or stock brokerage accounts. With these types of accounts, you name a person to receive any remaining funds in your checking, savings, or similar accounts at your death. The beneficiary has no right to funds while you are alive, and you can change the beneficiary at any time. The beneficiary named in the account receives the assets, not the beneficiary named in your Will.

In the case of co-owned property, such as real estate and cars, what happens to your share depends on the type of co-ownership.

- If you co-own the property as *tenants by the entirety* with your spouse, your share automatically goes to your spouse at your death. Your Will cannot supercede this law. This is how most married couples jointly own their homes.
- If you co-own property as *joint tenants,* the laws of most states provide that your share will be given to the surviving joint tenant at your death, not the beneficiary named in your Will.
- If you co-own the property as *tenants in common,* your share can be controlled by your Will and inherited by people other than the surviving tenants in common.

There is no need to probate assets that are not controlled by your Will. (Remember, probate is the court-supervised transfer of assets controlled by your Will.) The main way you can avoid probate is to own your assets during your lifetime in a way that allows your assets to pass at your death without being controlled by your Will.

Death and Taxes

Death and taxes are inexorably linked in many minds, but when it comes to your estate, there is good news. In 2005, the federal government only taxes estates of $1.5 million or more, with increased exemptions for the next several years. Thus, if your estate (including real estate equity and life insurance) totals less than $1.5 million, your beneficiaries can receive it free of federal estate taxes. States vary widely regarding estate taxes, but the state estate tax is far less than the federal estate tax levied on estates in excess of $1.5 million.

Addressing the Needs of Children

Yet another reason for having a Will is to provide for the care of any minor children you have. If you have minor children, part of your Will-making process will be to appoint a *guardian* in the event of the death of both parents. Should both parents die without a Will, the court will appoint a guardian for them until they reach legal majority (18 years of age in most states). The court considers what is in the best interests of the child, with great weight put on the parents' view of the person best suited to be guardian. The appropriate place for parents to express this view is in their Wills.

Should your spouse not be living, you will want to establish a *trust* to provide for your children financially until they become mature enough to responsibly manage their inheritance. In addition, you will want to select a *trustee* to manage your property for your children until they reach maturity.

With regards to anyone you name in your Will to serve a specific role—executor, guardian, or trustee—you should always name an additional person to serve as an alternate, should the first person you name be unable or unwilling to fulfill his or her role.

A Continuing Process

Perhaps you have already realized that you need to change your Will as your situation in life changes. You get married; you get divorced. Your children are minors; your children grow up. Even if you have a Will and your life situation does not change, over the years the people you have entrusted to carry out your wishes do change. They move away. They get sick. They also get older and may no longer feel capable of taking on new responsibilities.

Your Will should reflect your present needs. It is wise to review your Will, Power of Attorney for Finances, and Health Care Advance Directive every five years, or sooner, if major changes occur in your life.

A Conversation about Wills

People often voice the same concerns about the Will-making process. The following lawyer-client dialogue is similar to one that has taken place hundreds of times in every law office.

Client:
Why can't I just go home and write what I want done on a piece of paper? I've heard that handwritten Wills are just as good as other Wills.

Lawyer:
You're talking about a Holographic Will, which is not a good idea. Most states do not recognize Holographic Wills as valid, making your wishes as worthless as if you had not written anything at all. In some places, in some cases, they're legal. But why take a chance when you can use simplified forms that suit your needs?

Client:
Okay. But there's more to it than a simple form, isn't there?

Lawyer:
Well, there's a good reason for everything that's done. Each state protects you against fraud by specifying certain formalities. For instance, one of the most important requirements is having witnesses to your Will.

Client:
Oh, that's no problem.

Lawyer:
It can be a big one if the people you have in mind are not qualified under the law. A witness can't be someone who may benefit from the Will or someone who carries out its provisions. In other words, a witness has to be objective, with no personal stake in your financial affairs.

Client:
Well, that eliminates one of the people I had in mind! I don't see why I need any help saying what I want to do, though.

Lawyer:
You'd be surprised how tricky that can be. It's difficult to clearly state your intentions. Millions of lawsuits grow from badly written documents. It's simpler and safer when making your Will to talk in the court's language.

For example, someone making his or her own Will might write, "I leave everything to my children." Sounds clear enough—but the court will have several questions. Are all the children, regardless of their age, to receive the money? Do any of them need a guardian? If they do, who will give them their money and when? Those are just a few of the questions you'll need to answer and anticipate.

Client:
Can I leave my property to anyone I want to in my Will?

Lawyer:
Yes, within limits. You don't have to leave anything to your children, parents, brothers, or sisters. However, every state has a law protecting your spouse from disinheritance. Unless you and your spouse have signed a valid, written agreement waiving the right to share in each other's estate, your spouse has a legal right to a certain percentage of your estate. If your Will doesn't leave your spouse anything, the court will override it. A Will can't be used to violate the law.

Client:
What about community property?

Lawyer:
The concept of community property is of no great concern if you want your spouse to inherit all of your property. If you do not wish your spouse to receive all your property, do not use the simple Will forms. See a lawyer to draft a Will that specifically addresses your wishes.

Client:
Does my son-in-law or daughter-in-law get a share of my estate if my child is dead at the time of my death?

Lawyer:
No, not unless you specifically provide that your child's share goes to the child's spouse, or you specifically provide that the share of a deceased child goes to his or her estate. In this case, the share is part of the child's estate, and the distribution depends on his or her Will. Remember that it's highly likely your adult child has a Will with the spouse as the lead beneficiary.

Most people choose to leave the child's share to the child's living children (their grandchildren). That's pretty much the wisdom of the ages when it comes to assuring fairness and good feelings. All the Will forms (except the one intended for people who are neither married nor have children) contain the procedure for assuring that your estate goes to blood kin.

Client:
What if I get divorced?

Lawyer:
Whenever you have a major change in your life situation, you need to make a new Will. (See Chapter 7 for more information.)

Client:
Do my adopted children inherit the same as my biological children?

Lawyer:
Yes. Since you have legally adopted them, they are your children. Unless you provide a clause that specifically excludes them from inheriting, they have the same legal rights as your biological children. All of the Will forms state that your adopted children are considered the same as your biological children.

Client:
Does that mean my stepchildren inherit the same as my biological children?

Lawyer:
No. Unless the stepchildren are adopted, the law does not consider them to be your legal children. The Will forms do not leave any of your property to your stepchildren. If you want them to inherit a share of your estate, you need to specifically name them in the Will. In that case, you should see a lawyer. The same goes for the stepchildren of your children—they won't inherit a share of your deceased child's estate unless your Will specifically says so.

Client:
Do I have to list all of my personal stuff—my furniture, china, jewelry, books, etc.—in order to give it away in my Will?

Lawyer:
The Wills in this book leave all personal property to your spouse and then your children. Remember, your Will gives away what you own when you die, not what you own when you make the Will.

Client:
What happens to my Will when I die?

Lawyer:
Your executor must file the *original* Will with the court and ask the court to start the process of verifying the Will and setting up guidelines for probate. In this context, *original* means the Will form that you and your witnesses signed in ink—not a copy.

Client:
I know I need to pick a person I trust to be my executor, but I'd still feel more comfortable knowing there are checks and balances.

Lawyer:
Many people feel the same way. It helps to know that the court has strict rules to keep temptation at bay. For instance, in most states, the executor must file financial reports that are checked over by court auditors. He or she must also file receipts from your beneficiaries, vouching that they received monies given to them under your Will. Any executor who fails to file these receipts and financial reports can incur stiff penalties. These reports are very detailed, and probate court auditors can be sticklers about each element.

Often, professionals charging hourly rates (such as lawyers and accountants) have to be hired to prepare the reports because the executor hasn't the skill or experience. While probate procedures are designed to safeguard your estate from fraud or the negligence of your executor, these procedures can be time-consuming and expensive.

Client:
Can I avoid paying my bills by dying?

Lawyer:
The short answer is *no*! Every state has laws requiring your assets first be used to pay your debts before they go to your beneficiaries. Even if your Will does not have a provision telling your executor to pay your bills, these laws require your executor to pay all legitimate debts.

Client:
I suppose that includes taxes.

Lawyer:
You suppose correctly. If you owe income taxes for the year of your death, your executor must arrange for paying your taxes. People with large estates are well-advised to see an estate planner and minimize their heirs' estate tax burden. (This book is primarily for Americans with less than $1.5 million in assets, which includes most Americans.)

Client:
How do my funeral expenses get paid?

Lawyer:
Sometimes with difficulty. Most funeral homes at least require a deposit before the burial. Money that is owned in your own name will not be available to your family to bury you. It may be weeks before your executor can get official papers requiring your bank to release your funds. As you will see, your Financial Power of Attorney, which authorizes your agent to spend your money during your lifetime, ends at your death. Therefore, your agent can't pay funeral costs with your funds, either.

Some people prepay their funeral expenses or have a small, joint bank account with a child, with the understanding that the money is to be used for burial expenses. Any money that your executor or someone else spends can be repaid from your estate once the executor gets the official court papers allowing access to your money.

Client:
What does the sentence, "No bond should be required of my Executor," contained in the Wills mean?

Lawyer:
As part of the probate process, the court requires your executor to purchase a bond. If your executor steals your money and the money isn't in the accounts to pay your beneficiaries, then the bonding company would make these payments.

You can waive this requirement if you do not think your executor is likely to steal your money. (If you do, how wise would it be to appoint that person as your executor?) The waiver saves your estate the cost of the bond, which is expensive and usually unnecessary. The simple sentence, "No bond shall be required of my Executor or Trustee" takes care of the issue.

Client:
How important is it that my original Will be found?

Lawyer:
Very important. The court will only accept the original of your Will for probate. That means the Will must have your original signature, your witnesses' original signatures, and the notary public's signature and seal. The copies you make for reference or backup are not acceptable without an extensive court hearing to try and persuade the judge that you did not revoke this Will, and that a copy should be probated. Your original Will needs to be in a safe place, but it also needs to be accessible. (A safe deposit box may *not* be the best place to store your Will.) Make absolutely sure that the person you've named as executor knows where to find the original Will.

Client:
Okay, but where do I keep it? Let's say I put it in a box in my basement and the house burns down.

Lawyer:
You can't make any Will that protects you against all the zigs and zags of fate. Simply buy a fireproof box, and trust that your house will not burn down *with* neither the box nor you surviving. If the one in a million does happen, the court will straighten it all out, even if it does take time and money. All you can realistically do is take reasonable precautions.

Chapter 2:
Your Simple Will

Each Will form found in this book is accompanied with simple, straightforward instructions for completing it, a filled-in example, and a practice Will form to use as a draft, from which you will prepare the appropriate final forms. Choosing the form that is right for you depends on your particular life situation. Your life situation—marital status, children, and stage of life—places you in one of the following six categories:

1. married with adult children;
2. married with young children;
3. married without children;
4. unmarried with adult children;
5. unmarried with young children; or,
6. unmarried without children.

Until your circumstances change, you need not worry about any of the other Will forms. However, when it does change, you need to respond to your new situation.

Example: *John Smith is a single man who recently graduated from college. He makes a Will using Will Form 6, Unmarried without Children. Then he marries Mary, and each makes a Will using Will Form 3, Married without Children. Then they have two children a year apart, David and Ann. Now John and Mary each fill out Will Form 2, Married with Young Children. When David and Ann reach 21, John and Mary make new Wills, using Will Form 1, Married with Adult Children.*

If one spouse died, the other would fill out Will Form 4 or Will Form 5, Unmarried with Adult Children or Unmarried with Young Children, depending on the ages of David and Ann at the time of death.

Though the changes from Will form to Will form are not major, they are significant in carrying out your wishes. These variations are the reasons for providing a Will form to meet each of the basic situations.

Six Steps to Preparing Your Document

Now that you have reviewed the six life situations and have seen an example of how each could be relevant at various times in your life, you are ready to select the appropriate forms you need to complete. The remainder of this chapter covers your Will form, which is generally the most complicated of the documents. However, you will find it useful to follow these steps covering the entire process.

◆ **STEP 1.** Think about which of the simple Wills fits your situation at this time. Look at the information the form requires. Since you already know most of the needed information (for example, your name and address), getting this information together should not be difficult. However, because you name executors, and possibly guardians and trustees, you will have to ask them to serve. In order to ask them, you will have to know what each activity will demand of them. You also have to arrange for witnesses to the Will and a notary public.

◆ **STEP 2.** Read the instructions for your selected Will form and study the sample completed form. Then, fill in the draft copy provided and tinker with it until you are satisfied with what you have.

◆ **STEP 3.** In the Appendix, you will find the form to which you will copy your draft.

NOTE: *Just completing in the blanks on the paper form does not fulfill the legal requirements for a valid Will. Use the completed form to type a new document—that will be your original Will when signed by you and your witnesses, and notarized. Your Will should not have any corrections or erasures—this helps protect against a fraudulent Will. The accompanying CD-ROM contains the blank Will documents, making this easy to do.*

◆ **STEP 4.** Go to Chapter 3. Carefully read about the *Self-Proving Affidavit* that will be attached to your Will. Additional information will explain the process for completing the task.

◆ **STEP 5.** The next document you should complete is the *Health Care Advance Directive*, which incorporates the provisions of a *Living Will* and a *Power of Attorney for Health Care*. Turn to Chapter 4 and review the form carefully—you will be deciding whom you trust to make life-or-death decisions when you are critically or terminally ill. Review the sample form and then complete your own.

◆ **STEP 6.** When you have completed your Will form, Self-Proving Affidavit, and Health Care Advance Directive, go to Chapter 5 and read the section, *Financial Power of Attorney*—another critical document you should have in the event of your incapacitation. Make a note of the decisions you need to make. Review the sample forms and then complete your own.

NOTE: *Since all of the documents require witnesses and a notary, save yourself time and complete all final documents at the same time.*

These forms should make planning for your future a relatively simple matter. If you think that none of the forms fit your situation, please review the section in the Introduction, "When Not to Use This Book."

Married with Adult Children (Will Form 1)

Use Will Form 1, *Married with Adult Children,* if you are married, all your children are adults, and you wish the following things to happen upon your death.

❑ Your spouse inherits your entire estate.

❑ If you outlive your spouse, your adult children (including adopted children) inherit your estate in equal shares.

❑ If one or more of your children dies before you do, that child's children (your grandchildren) inherit your dead child's portion, in equal shares.

❑ If your dead child has no living children, your living children inherit the dead child's portion, in equal shares.

❑ If any grandchildren inherit your estate because of a dead child and the grandchildren are young, the portion of your estate your grandchildren inherit is held in trust until they reach an age you select.

❑ Your spouse is your executor.

❑ You select an alternate executor to serve if you outlive your spouse.

❑ You select a trustee and an alternate trustee for your Grandchild's Trust.

❑ You waive the requirement that your executor and trustee post a bond.

❑ You give your executor and trustee the authority to wind up your financial affairs, including the distribution of your property to your family.

An Example of Married with Adult Children

The sample, filled-in form on page 17 shows how a *Married with Adult Children* Will form works. It is based on the following situation.

John Smith is married to Mary Smith. They have two children, David (26) and Ann (24). David, an investment banker, is married and has three children—Sarah (8), Susie (6), and Ricky (4). Ann, a nurse, is married and now goes by the name Anne Jones. She has one child—Katherine (2). John wants Mary to inherit all of his property and to be his executor. If John outlives Mary, he wants his children to inherit equal 50% shares of his property. If David predeceases him, John wants David's three children to split equally the 50% share of his estate that David would have inherited if David had outlived him. If Ann predeceases him, John wants Ann's child to inherit the 50% share of his estate that Ann would have inherited if she had outlived him. If any of his grandchildren inherit from him because of the death of a parent, John wants the grandchild's share of his estate kept in trust until the grandchild reaches the age of 21 (Grandchild's Trust). John wants David to be his alternate executor. He wants his surviving child to be trustee of the Grandchild's Trust.

SAMPLE, FILLED-IN WILL FORM 1
Married with Adult Children

Will of _____John Smith_____

I, _____John Smith_____ of _____Any Town, Any State_____,
make this my Will. I revoke any other Wills and codicils made by me.

1. Family

I am married to _____Mary Smith_____, my spouse. I have ___2___
children, _____David Smith and Ann Jones_____, my children. The term
"my children" includes the aforementioned children, all children born after the making of this Will,
and all children adopted by me.

2. Residuary Estate

A. I give my residuary estate, that is, all of my property, real, personal, and mixed, of whatever kind and wherever situated, of which I may die possessed, to my spouse, _____Mary Smith_____, if my spouse survives me.

B. If my spouse does not survive me, I leave this residuary estate, in equal shares, to my children.

C. If a child does not survive me, then the deceased child's share devolves, in equal shares, to the deceased child's children. If none of the deceased child's children survive me, then this share devolves, in equal shares, to my surviving children.

D. If a deceased child's children are entitled to a share of my estate, I leave this bequest to my trustee to be held in trust under Article 4, "Grandchild's Trust."

3. Appointment of Fiduciaries

A. Executor. I appoint my spouse to serve as my executor. If my spouse cannot serve, then I appoint _____David Smith_____ to serve as my executor.

B. Trustee. I appoint _____David Smith_____ to serve as my trustee. If _____David Smith_____ cannot serve, then I appoint _____Ann Jones_____ to serve as my trustee.

C. No bond shall be required of my executor or trustee.

4. Grandchild's Trust

My trustee shall hold the assets passing to my grandchildren in a separate trust for each grandchild under this article until that grandchild has reached the age of ___21___ years, the termination date.

A. Until the termination date, my trustee shall distribute to or for the benefit of my grandchild as much of the net income and principal as my trustee may consider appropriate for the grandchild's health, education, support, or maintenance, annually adding to principal any undistributed income.

B. Upon the termination date, my trustee shall distribute the remaining assets to the grandchild.

5. Miscellaneous

My executor and trustee shall exercise all powers conferred by law, in addition to the following powers, which are to be exercised in the best interest of my estate or trust.

A. To hold and retain any property owned by me.

B. To sell, exchange, or lease any property.

C. To vote stock; to convert securities belonging to my estate into other securities; and, to exercise all other rights and privileges of a person owning similar properties.

D. To settle claims.

E. To pay all debts and taxes.

F. To do all other acts necessary for the proper management, investment, and distribution of my estate or trust.

G. To take all actions to have the probate of this Will conducted as free of court supervision as possible.

I have signed this Will in the presence of the undersigned witnesses on this __18th__ day of _____January_____, 20_06_, at _____Any Town_____, State of _____Any State_____, and declare it is my Will, that I signed it willingly, that I executed it as my free and voluntary act for the purpose expressed herein, and that I am of legal age and sound mind.

John Smith
[Signature]

[Signatures of witnesses not provided.]

Initials: ___*JS*___ ___*W1*___ ___*W2*___ ___*W3*___   Page _2_ of _2_
Testator   Witness   Witness   Witness

Continuing the Conversation about Will Form 1

Client:

I just want to make sure I understand the legalese. My spouse gets everything I own if my spouse outlives me. The children inherit equally from me only if I outlive my spouse. Correct?

Lawyer:

Yes. Articles 2.A and B make this clear.

> Article 2.A. I give my residuary estate, that is, all of my property, real, personal, and mixed, of whatever kind and wherever situated, of which I may die possessed, to my spouse, Mary Smith, if my spouse survives me.

> Article 2.B. If my spouse does not survive me, I leave this residuary estate, in equal shares, to my children.

Client:

And my grandchildren do not inherit anything from me if all of my children are alive at my death?

Lawyer:

Correct. The only time a grandchild would inherit from you is if your child, their parent, died before you. The dead child's share would be split equally between that dead child's children. For example, if David died, his 50% share would be split equally between his three children. If Ann died, her 50% share would be given to her only child. If David and Ann both outlived John, they would each inherit 50% of his estate.

Client:

In case my spouse dies first, which of my grown children should I name my alternate executor?

Lawyer:

People often wrestle with this question. It is best to appoint just one of your children as executor. It saves a lot of paperwork. If you have two executors, you have to get two signatures on checks, court papers, etc. It's administratively easier with a single executor. Some parents name the child who lives the closest to them, thinking the duties of executor would be less burdensome on the geographically close child. Some parents make their decision based on the child who is better with finances, since the executor's duties are primarily financial. John chooses his investment banker son, David, to be alternate executor. If you are concerned with family harmony, you might consider discussing your decision, and the reasons for it, with all of your children while you can.

Client:
Who should I make trustee? I want to keep this job in the family.

Lawyer:
The Grandchild's Trust only comes into existence if your spouse and one of your children die before you. The trustee's job is to manage the money going to your underage grandchild. The trustee obviously will have nothing to do with the custody of the grandchild. I recommend picking the child you think is the best money manger as primary trustee, and the child who is the next best money manager, alternate trustee. John chooses his investment banker son, David, to be primary trustee and nurse daughter, Ann, to be alternate trustee.

Client:
What does the grandchild's trustee have to do?

Lawyer:
The grandchild's trustee has to manage the money in the trust until the grandchild reaches the age you have selected. John Smith selected 21 years of age. If wife Mary and daughter Ann were both dead at John's death, son David would be trustee for Ann's daughter's (Katherine) 50% share of John's estate. Trustee David would invest the trust funds and decide the amount of trust funds to be given to Katherine's guardian (probably her father) for Katherine's benefit. Trust funds could be used for Katherine's health, education, support, and maintenance expenses. When Katherine turns 21, David would have to give her any money remaining in the trust fund.

Instructions for Completing the Draft Will Form 1—Married with Adult Children

Put together the following information:

1. Your name.
2. Your city and state.
3. Your spouse's name.
4. The number of children you have.
5. Your child's (or children's) name(s).
6. Your alternate executor's name.
7. Your trustee's name (you will fill in this name in the blanks of the draft two times).
8. Your alternate for trustee's name.
9. The age at which your grandchildren must receive their inheritances.
10. The date you will sign your Will.
11. The city and state where you sign your Will.
12. Your initials.
13. Your witnesses' initials.

Now you are ready to fill in your draft form. Fill in your information next to the numbered blank in the draft. Your draft is the place for you to experiment, to make and correct errors. You do not want erasures on your Will. It may be a good idea to live with the draft of your Will for a few days before filling out your final Will. Do not sign the draft. When you are ready, continue to Chapter 3 to create your Self-Proving Affidavit, and then to Chapter 6, which contains instructions for preparing and signing your Will. Do not forget to prepare your Living Will (Chapter 4) and Power of Attorney (Chapter 5). It is easy to complete these two documents while you have the witnesses and notary present for the signing of your Will.

Draft
Married with Adult Children

Will of (1)_____

I, (1)_____ of (2)_____,
make this my Will. I revoke any other Wills and codicils made by me.

1. Family

I am married to (3)_____, my spouse. I have
(4)_____ children, (5)_____, my chil-
dren. The term "my children" includes the aforementioned children, all children born after the making of this Will, and all children adopted by me.

2. Residuary Estate

A. I give my residuary estate, that is, all of my property, real, personal, and mixed, of what-
    ever kind and wherever situated, of which I may die possessed, to my spouse,
    (3)_____, if my spouse survives me.
B. If my spouse does not survive me, I leave this residuary estate, in equal shares, to my
    children.
C. If a child does not survive me, then the deceased child's share devolves, in equal shares,
    to the deceased child's children. If none of the deceased child's children survive me, then
    this share devolves, in equal shares, to my surviving children.
D. If a deceased child's children are entitled to a share of my estate, I leave this bequest to
    my trustee to be held in trust under Article 4, "Grandchild's Trust."

3. Appointment of Fiduciaries

A. Executor. I appoint my spouse to serve as my executor. If my spouse cannot serve, then
    I appoint (6)_____ to serve as my
    executor.
B. Trustee. I appoint (7)_____ to serve
    as my trustee. If (7)_____ cannot serve,
    then I appoint (8)_____ to serve as my trustee.
C. No bond shall be required of my executor or trustee.

4. Grandchild's Trust

My trustee shall hold the assets passing to my grandchildren in a separate trust for each grandchild under this article until that grandchild has reached the age of (9)_____ years, the termination date.

A. Until the termination date, my trustee shall distribute to or for the benefit of my grandchild as much of the net income and principal as my trustee may consider appropriate for the grandchild's health, education, support, or maintenance, annually adding to principal any undistributed income.

B. Upon the termination date, my trustee shall distribute the remaining assets to the grandchild.

5. Miscellaneous

My executor and trustee shall exercise all powers conferred by law, in addition to the following powers, which are to be exercised in the best interest of my estate or trust.

A. To hold and retain any property owned by me.

B. To sell, exchange, or lease any property.

C. To vote stock; to convert securities belonging to my estate into other securities; and, to exercise all other rights and privileges of a person owning similar properties.

D. To settle claims.

E. To pay all debts and taxes.

F. To do all other acts necessary for the proper management, investment, and distribution of my estate or trust.

G. To take all actions to have the probate of this Will conducted as free of court supervision as possible.

I have signed this Will in the presence of the undersigned witnesses on this (10)_____ day of _____, 20_____, at (11)_____, State of (11)_____, and declare it is my Will, that I signed it willingly, that I executed it as my free and voluntary act for the purpose expressed herein, and that I am of legal age and sound mind.

[Do Not Sign]_____
[Signature]

[Signatures of witnesses not provided.]

Married with Young Children (Will Form 2)

Use Will Form 2, *Married with Young Children*, if you are married and *any* of your children are young. Even if you also have adult children (with possible children of their own), you still use this form if any of your children are young. If you outlive your spouse, this form keeps all of your property in trust for the benefit of all of your children, until your youngest child reaches an age you select. Use this form if you wish the following to happen upon your death.

❑ Your spouse inherits your entire estate.

❑ If you outlive your spouse and all of your children (including adopted children) are adults at your death, your adult children inherit your estate in equal portions.

❑ If you outlive your spouse and one or more of your children are young at your death, your entire estate will be held in a *Children's Trust* until your youngest child reaches the age you select (usually 21). Money from this trust can be spent on all of your children during the life of the trust. The trust ends when your youngest child reaches the age you select (usually 21). When it ends, any property in the trust is distributed equally to all of your children.

❑ You select a guardian and an alternate guardian to care for your minor children if you outlive your spouse.

❑ If one or more of your children is dead at your death, leaving children, that dead child's children (your grandchildren) inherit your dead child's portion, in equal shares.

❑ If your dead child has no living children, your living children inherit the dead child's portion, in equal shares.

❑ If any grandchildren inherit your estate because of a dead child, and the grandchildren are young, the portion of your estate your grandchildren inherit is held in trust until they reach the age you select (*Grandchild's Trust*).

❑ Your spouse is your executor.

❑ You select an alternate executor to serve if you outlive your spouse.

❑ You select a trustee and an alternate trustee for your Children's Trust and for your Grandchildren's Trust.

❑ You waive the requirement that your executor and trustee post a bond.

❑ You give your executor and trustee the authority to wind up your financial affairs, including the distribution of your property to your family.

An Example of Married with Young Children

The sample, filled-in form exemplifies how a *Married with Young Children* Will form works. It is based on the following situation.

John Smith is married to Mary Smith. They have two children, David (18) and Ann (12). John wants Mary to inherit all of his property and to be his executor. If John outlives Mary and dies before Ann is 21, he wants all of his property held in trust for the benefit of both children until Ann reaches 21, when the money is given outright, in equal shares, to both children. If a child dies during the course of this trust, the surviving child will be given all of the money. If John outlives Mary and Ann is 21 at John's death, he wants his children to inherit equal shares (50%/50%) of his property, outright and free of trust. If a child dies leaving children, John wants the dead child's children to inherit equal shares of the dead child's portion of his estate. If a grandchild inherits because of the death of his child, John wants the grandchild's share of his estate kept in trust until the grandchild reaches the age of 21 (Grandchild's Trust). John wants his accountant brother, Harry Smith, to be his alternate executor and trustee. John wants Mary's sister, Nancy Evans, to be guardian with custody of his minor children. If Nancy cannot be guardian, he wants Harry to be guardian. If Harry cannot be trustee, he wants Nancy to be trustee.

Married with Young Children

SAMPLE, FILLED-IN WILL FORM 2
Married with Young Children

Will of _____John Smith_____

I, _____John Smith_____ of _____Any Town, Any State_____,
make this my Will. I revoke any other Wills and codicils made by me.

1. Family

I am married to _____Mary Smith_____, my spouse. I have __2__
children, _____David Smith and Ann Smith_____, my children. The term
"my children" includes the aforementioned children, all children born after the making of this Will,
and all children adopted by me.

2. Residuary Estate

A. I give my residuary estate, that is, all of my property, real, personal, and mixed, of what-
    ever kind and wherever situated, of which I may die possessed, to my spouse,
    _____Mary Smith_____, if my spouse survives me.

B. If my spouse does not survive me, I leave this residuary estate to my children. If my
    youngest child has, on the date of my death, reached the age of __21__ years, I leave this
    residuary estate outright to my children, in equal shares. If my youngest child has not,
    on the date of my death, reached the age of __21__ years, I leave this residuary estate to
    my trustee to be held in trust under Article 4, "Children's Trust."

C   If a child does not survive me and no "Children's Trust" is created according to Article 2.B
    above, then the deceased child's share devolves, in equal shares, to the deceased child's chil-
    dren. If none of the deceased child's children survive me, then this share devolves, in equal
    shares, to my surviving children.

D. If a deceased child's children are entitled to a share of my estate, I leave this bequest to
    my trustee to be held in trust under Article 5, "Grandchild's Trust."

3. Appointment of Fiduciaries

A. Executor. I appoint my spouse to serve as my executor. If my spouse cannot serve, then
    I appoint _____Harry Smith_____ to serve as my executor.

B. Guardian. If, at my death, any of my children are minors and a guardian is needed for my minor children, I appoint _____Nancy Evans_____ to serve as my guardian. If _____Nancy Evans_____ cannot serve, then I appoint _____Harry Smith_____ to serve as my guardian.

C. Trustee. I appoint _____Harry Smith_____ to serve as my trustee. If _____Harry Smith_____ cannot serve, then I appoint _____Nancy Evans_____ to serve as my trustee.

D. No bond shall be required of my executor, trustee, or guardian.

4. Children's Trust

If a "Children's Trust" is created according to Article 2.B above, my trustee shall hold the assets passing to my children in trust under this article.

A. Until the termination date, my trustee shall distribute to or for the benefit of my children as much of the net income and principal as my trustee may consider appropriate for their health, education, support, or maintenance, annually adding to principal any undistributed income. My trustee may distribute income and principal unequally, and may distribute to some children and not to others. My trustee may consider other income and assets readily available to my children in making distributions.

B. Upon the termination date, my trustee shall distribute the remaining assets, in equal shares, to my surviving children.

C. The termination date is the date on which my youngest living child reaches the age of __21__ years.

5. Grandchild's Trust

My trustee shall hold the assets passing to my grandchildren in a separate trust for each grandchild under this article until that grandchild has reached the age of __21__ years, the termination date.

A. Until the termination date, my trustee shall distribute to or for the benefit of my grandchild as much of the net income and principal as my trustee may consider appropriate for the grandchild's health, education, support, or maintenance, annually adding to principal any undistributed income.

B. Upon the termination date, my trustee shall distribute the remaining assets to the grandchild.

6. Miscellaneous

My executor and trustee shall exercise all powers conferred by law, in addition to the following powers, which are to be exercised in the best interest of my estate or trust.

A. To hold and retain any property owned by me.
B. To sell, exchange, or lease any property.
C. To vote stock; to convert securities belonging to my estate into other securities; and, to exercise all other rights and privileges of a person owning similar properties.
D. To settle claims.
E. To pay all debts and taxes.
F. To do all other acts necessary for the proper management, investment, and distribution of my estate or trust.
G. To take all actions to have the probate of this Will conducted as free of court supervision as possible.

I have signed this Will in the presence of the undersigned witnesses on this __18th__ day of ___January___, 20_06_, at ___Any Town___, State of ___Any State___, and declare it is my Will, that I signed it willingly, that I executed it as my free and voluntary act for the purpose expressed herein, and that I am of legal age and sound mind.

___*John Smith*___
[Signature]

[Signatures of witnesses not provided.]

Continuing the Conversation about Will Form 2

Client:

I just want to make sure I understand the legalese. My spouse gets everything I own if my spouse outlives me? My children inherit from me only if I outlive my spouse?

Lawyer:

Correct. Article 2.A and B make this clear.

> Article 2.A. I give my residuary estate, that is, all of my property, real, personal, and mixed, of whatever kind and wherever situated, of which I may die possessed, to my spouse, Mary Smith, if my spouse survives me.
>
> Article 2.B. If my spouse does not survive me, I leave this residuary estate to my children. If my youngest child has, on the date of my death, reached the age of 21 years, I leave this residuary estate outright to my children, in equal shares. If my youngest child has not, on the date of my death, reached the age of 21 years, I leave this residuary estate to my trustee to be held in trust under Article 4, "Children's Trust."

Client:

And my grandchildren do not inherit anything from me if all of my children are alive at my death?

Lawyer:

Correct. The only time a grandchild would inherit from you is if your child—their parent—died before you. The dead child's share would be split equally among that dead child's children. For example, if David was dead at John's death, leaving three children, his 50% share would be split equally among his three children. If Ann was dead at John's death, leaving one child, her 50% share would be given to her only child. If David and Ann both outlived John, they would each inherit 50% of his estate.

Client:
Can you explain the Children's Trust?

Lawyer:
If you outlive your spouse and one of your children is under an age you select, everything you own goes into a Children's Trust. If John outlives Mary and dies when daughter Ann is 12 and son David is 18, all of John's property goes into a Children Trust, managed by brother Harry for nine years, until Ann turns 21. Trustee Harry can spend trust funds on both Ann and David during these nine years and does not have to spend equal amounts on each child. The Children's Trust allows the trustee the same flexibility that parents have to spend more on one child, as circumstances dictate, than another child.

It is better for parents not to try to rule from the grave, as unexpected things happen. For example, one child may have greater medical or educational expenses than another. You should make sure that your trustee understands your wishes for your children. When Ann becomes 21, she and David are entitled to split equally whatever remains of the trust fund. So, equality per child principle is maintained after both children have reached 21.

NOTE: *If a child dies in the course of this trust and has children, your surviving child—not your grandchildren—inherits the dead child's portion of the Children's Trust.*

Client:
My children are young now. Why am I worrying about a Grandchild's Trust?

Lawyer:
Your Will governs circumstances present when you die, not when you make it. Hopefully, John will still be alive in forty years, when his children are 52 and 58, with teenagers of their own. If son David dies before John, and has his own children, John wants David's children to inherit equally David's share. But the grandchildren would not inherit until they reached 21. Their share would be kept in trust—the Grandchild's Trust.

Client:
What does the trustee of the Children's Trust have to do?

Lawyer:
The trustee manages the trust funds for the life of the trust. The trustee also has the discretion to decide how much of the trust funds should be spent on which child. Trust funds can be spent on health, education, maintenance, and support expenses of the children. But the trustee does not have personal custody and control over your children—that responsibility falls to their guardian. Trustee Harry and the Guardian Nancy would confer on the needs of the children and Trustee Harry would give Guardian Nancy money to be spent on the children.

Client:
What does the guardian do?

Lawyer:
The guardian has custody of your children until they reach legal majority, which is 18 years of age in most states. The person you name as guardian of your children must, in most states, also be appointed by the courts. The judge pays attention to the parents' wishes as to guardian. The Will of the parents is the place the judge looks to find the parents' wishes. The judge considers the best interest of the child in making the guardian appointment.

Client:
Under the Children's Trust, my oldest child would not get money from my estate until my youngest child reached an age I select. Correct?

Lawyer:
Correct. All of your property is held in trust until your youngest child reaches an age your select. But remember, an older child can receive money from the trustee. It's just that the older child has no right to receive his or her remaining principal share until the youngest reaches the age you select.

Client:
What does the trustee of the Grandchild's Trust have to do?

Lawyer:
The grandchild's trustee has to manage the money in the Grandchild's Trust until the grandchild reaches the age you have selected. John Smith selected the age of 21, at which time the trustee must give the grandchild any money remaining in the grandchild's trust fund.

Instructions for Completing the Draft Will Form 2—Married with Young Children

Gather the following information:

1. Your name.
2. Your city and state.
3. Your spouse's name.
4. The number of children you have.
5. Your child or children's name(s).
6. The age that your youngest child must reach in order for all your children to receive their inheritance outright (without a trust). You will fill in the age in the blanks of the draft three times.
7. Your alternate executor's name.
8. Your guardian's name. You will fill in this name in the blanks of the draft two times.
9. Your alternate guardian's name.
10. Your trustee's name. You will fill in this name in the blanks of the draft two times.
11. Your alternate trustee's name.
12. The age at which any grandchild must receive his or her inheritance.
13. The date you will sign your Will.
14. The city and state where you sign your Will.
15. Your initials.
16. Your witnesses' initials.

Now you are ready to fill in your draft form. Fill in your information next to the numbered blank in the draft. Your draft is the place for you to experiment, to make and correct errors. You do not want erasures on your Will. It may be a good idea to live with the draft of your Will for a few days before filling out your final Will. Do not sign the draft. When you are ready, continue on to Chapter 3 to create your Self-Proving Affidavit, and then on to Chapter 6, which contains instructions for preparing and signing your Will. Do not forget to prepare your Living Will (Chapter 4) and Power of Attorney (Chapter 5). It is easy to complete these two documents while you have the witnesses and notary present for the signing of your Will.

Married with Young Children

Draft
Married with Young Children

Will of (1)_____

I, (1)_____ of (2)_____,
make this my Will. I revoke any other Wills and codicils made by me.

1. Family

I am married to (3)_____, my spouse. I have (4)_____
children, (5)_____, my children. The
term "my children" includes the aforementioned children, all children born after the making of this
Will, and all children adopted by me.

2. Residuary Estate

A. I give my residuary estate, that is, all of my property, real, personal, and mixed, of what-
    ever kind and wherever situated, of which I may die possessed, to my spouse,
    (3)_____, if my spouse survives me.

B. If my spouse does not survive me, I leave this residuary estate to my children. If my
    youngest child has, on the date of my death, reached the age of (6)_____ years, I leave
    this residuary estate outright to my children, in equal shares. If my youngest child has
    not, on the date of my death, reached the age of (6)_____ years, I leave this residuary
    estate to my trustee to be held in trust under Article 4, "Children's Trust."

C   If a child does not survive me and no "Children's Trust" is created according to Article 2.B
    above, then the deceased child's share devolves, in equal shares, to the deceased child's chil-
    dren. If none of the deceased child's children survive me, then this share devolves, in equal
    shares, to my surviving children.

D. If a deceased child's children are entitled to a share of my estate, I leave this bequest to
    my trustee to be held in trust under Article 5, "Grandchild's Trust."

3. Appointment of Fiduciaries

A. Executor. I appoint my spouse to serve as my executor. If my spouse cannot serve, then
    I appoint (7)_____ to serve as my executor.

B. Guardian. If, at my death, any of my children are minors and a guardian is needed for my minor children, I appoint (8)_____ to serve as my guardian. If (8)_____ cannot serve, then I appoint (9)_____ to serve as my guardian.

C. Trustee. I appoint (10)_____ to serve as my trustee. If (10)_____ cannot serve, then I appoint (11)_____ to serve as my trustee.

D. No bond shall be required of my executor, trustee, or guardian.

4. Children's Trust

If a "Children's Trust" is created according to Article 2.B above, my trustee shall hold the assets passing to my children in trust under this article.

A. Until the termination date, my trustee shall distribute to or for the benefit of my children as much of the net income and principal as my trustee may consider appropriate for their health, education, support, or maintenance, annually adding to principal any undistributed income. My trustee may distribute income and principal unequally, and may distribute to some children and not to others. My trustee may consider other income and assets readily available to my children in making distributions.

B. Upon the termination date, my trustee shall distribute the remaining assets, in equal shares, to my surviving children.

C. The termination date is the date on which my youngest living child reaches the age of (6)_____ years.

5. Grandchild's Trust

My trustee shall hold the assets passing to my grandchildren in a separate trust for each grandchild under this article until that grandchild has reached the age of (12)_____ years, the termination date.

A. Until the termination date, my trustee shall distribute to or for the benefit of my grandchild as much of the net income and principal as my trustee may consider appropriate for the grandchild's health, education, support, or maintenance, annually adding to principal any undistributed income.

B. Upon the termination date, my trustee shall distribute the remaining assets to the grandchild.

6. Miscellaneous

My executor and trustee shall exercise all powers conferred by law, in addition to the following powers, which are to be exercised in the best interest of my estate or trust.

A. To hold and retain any property owned by me.

B. To sell, exchange, or lease any property.

C. To vote stock; to convert securities belonging to my estate into other securities; and, to exercise all other rights and privileges of a person owning similar properties.

D. To settle claims.

E. To pay all debts and taxes.

F. To do all other acts necessary for the proper management, investment, and distribution of my estate or trust.

G. To take all actions to have the probate of this Will conducted as free of court supervision as possible.

I have signed this Will in the presence of the undersigned witnesses on this (13)_____ day of _____, 20_____, at (14)_____, State of (14)_____, and declare it is my Will, that I signed it willingly, that I executed it as my free and voluntary act for the purpose expressed herein, and that I am of legal age and sound mind.

[Do Not Sign] _____
[Signature]

[Signatures of witnesses not provided.]

Married without Children (Will Form 3)

Use Will Form 3 if you are *Married without Children* and you wish the following to happen upon your death.

- ❏ Your spouse inherits your entire estate.
- ❏ If you outlive your spouse, your property goes to whomever you name in your Will.
- ❏ If any of your beneficiaries are young, your gift is held in trust until they reach an age you select.
- ❏ Your spouse is your executor.
- ❏ You select an alternate executor to serve if you outlive your spouse.
- ❏ You select a trustee and an alternate trustee for any young beneficiary's trust.
- ❏ You waive the requirement that your executor and trustee post a bond.
- ❏ You give your executor and trustee the authority to wind up your financial affairs, including the distribution of your property to your beneficiaries.

An Example of Married without Children

The sample, filled-in form on page 38 shows how the *Married without Children* Will form works. It is based on the following situation.

John Smith is married to Mary Smith. They have no children. John wants Mary to inherit all of his property and to be his executor. If John outlives Mary, he wants his brother Paul Smith to inherit half of his property, and Mary's two sisters, Sally Davis and Nancy Evans, to each inherit a 25% portion of his property. Paul and Sally both have children. Nancy has no children. If Paul or Sally should die before him, John wants their children to inherit the share that their parent would have inherited. If Nancy dies before him, he wants Sally, or her children, to inherit Nancy's share. If any beneficiary is under age 21, John wants the young person's share of his estate to be held in trust until the young person reaches the age of 21. John wants his brother Paul to be his alternate executor and trustee of the Young Person's Trust. If Paul cannot be trustee, he wants Sally to be trustee.

SAMPLE, FILLED-IN WILL FORM 3
Married without Children

Will of ___John Smith___

I, _____John Smith_____ of _____Any Town, Any State_____,
make this my Will. I revoke any other Wills and codicils made by me.

1. Family

I am married to _____Mary Smith_____.

2. Residuary Estate

A. I give my residuary estate, that is, all of my property, real, personal, and mixed, of whatever kind and wherever situated, of which I may die possessed, to my spouse, _____Mary Smith_____, if my spouse survives me.

B. If my spouse does not survive me, I leave my residuary estate to the following:

   1. 50% to my brother, Paul Smith, if he survives me. If he does not survive me, this bequest is given to his children who survive me, in equal shares.

   2. 25% to Sally Davis, if she survives me. If she does not survive me, this bequest is given to her children who survive me, in equal shares.

   3. 25% to Nancy Evans, if she survives me. If she does not survive me, this bequest is given to Sally Davis, if she survives me. If Sally Davis does not survive me, this bequest is given to the children of Sally Davis who survive me, in equal shares.

3. Appointment of Fiduciaries

A. Executor. I appoint my spouse to serve as my executor. If my spouse cannot serve, then I appoint _____Paul Smith_____ to serve as my executor.

B. Trustee. I appoint _____Paul Smith_____ to serve as my trustee. If _____Paul Smith_____ cannot serve, then I appoint _____Sally Davis_____ to serve as my trustee.

C. No bond shall be required of my executor, or trustee.

Initials: _*JS*_   _*W1*_   _*W2*_   _*W3*_   Page _1_ of _2_
          Testator Witness Witness Witness

4. Young Person's Trust

My trustee shall hold the assets passing to young persons in a separate trust for each young person under this article until that young person has reached the age of __21__ years, the termination date.

    A. Until the termination date, my trustee shall distribute to or for the benefit of the young person as much of the net income and principal as my trustee may consider appropriate for the young person's health, education, support, or maintenance, annually adding to principal any undistributed income.

    B. Upon the termination date, my trustee shall distribute the remaining assets to the young person.

5. Miscellaneous

My executor shall exercise all powers conferred by law, in addition to the following powers, which are to be exercised in the best interest of my estate or trust.

    A. To hold and retain any property owned by me.

    B. To sell, exchange, or lease any property.

    C. To vote stock; to convert securities belonging to my estate into other securities; and, to exercise all other rights and privileges of a person owning similar properties.

    D. To settle claims.

    E. To pay all debts and taxes.

    F. To do all other acts necessary for the proper management, investment, and distribution of my estate or trust.

    G. To take all actions to have the probate of this Will conducted as free of court supervision as possible.

I have signed this Will in the presence of the undersigned witnesses on this __18th__ day of _____ January _____ , 20 __06__ , at _____ Any Town _____ , State of _____ Any State _____ , and declare it is my Will, that I signed it willingly, that I executed it as my free and voluntary act for the purpose expressed herein, and that I am of legal age and sound mind.

_____ *John Smith* _____
[Signature]

[Signatures of witnesses not provided.]

Married without Children

Continuing the Conversation about Will Form 3

Client:
I just want to make sure I understand the legalese. My spouse gets everything I own if my spouse outlives me. Correct?

Lawyer:
Correct. Article 2.A leaves everything to your spouse.

> Article 2.A. I give my residuary estate, that is, all of my property, real, personal, and mixed, of whatever kind and wherever situated, of which I may die possessed, to my spouse, Mary Smith, if my spouse survives me.

Client:
What are important things to make sure of in this?

Lawyer:
You need to remember that your Will isn't valid until you are dead. Make sure you specify who gets your property if the people you name in your Will are dead. The law has phrases that accomplish this if you have children. But if you don't have children, you need to specify whether your gift goes to the children of your beneficiary. If you do not want your gift to go to the children of your beneficiary, you must state who you want to get the gift.

Client:
What does the trustee for young persons trust have to do?

Lawyer:
The young person's trustee has to manage the money in the Young Person's Trust until the young person reaches an age you select. John Smith selected 21 years of age. His trustee, Paul, would invest the trust funds and decide how much of the trust should be given to the young person for health, education, maintenance, and support expenses. When the young person reaches the age of 21, Paul would have to give the young person any money remaining in the trust fund.

Instructions for Completing the Draft Will Form 3—Married without Children

Put together the following information:

1. Your name.
2. Your city and state.
3. Your spouse's name.
4. A list of those who you wish to receive your estate if your spouse is not alive. If you do not want these beneficiaries' children to receive your gift if your beneficiary predeceases you, you must state who is to receive your gift.
5. Your alternate executor's name.
6. Your trustee's name. You will fill this name in the blanks of the draft two times.
7. Your alternate trustee's name.
8. The age at which young beneficiaries must receive their inheritance.
9. The date you will sign your Will.
10. The city and state where you sign your Will.
11. Your initials.
12. Your witnesses' initials.

Now you are ready to fill in your draft form. Fill in your information next to the numbered blank in the draft. Your draft is the place for you to experiment, to make and correct errors. You do not want erasures on your Will. It may be a good idea to live with the draft of your Will for a few days before filling out your final Will. Do not sign the draft. When you are ready, continue on to Chapter 3 to create your Self-Proving Affidavit, and then on to Chapter 6, which contains instructions for preparing and signing your Will. Do not forget to prepare your Living Will (Chapter 4) and Power of Attorney (Chapter 5). It is easy to complete these two documents while you have the witnesses and notary present for the signing of your Will.

Married without Children

Draft
Married without Children

Will of (1)_____

I, (1)_____ of (2)_____,
make this my Will. I revoke any other Wills and codicils made by me.

1. Family

I am married to (3)_____.

2. Residuary Estate

A. I give my residuary estate, that is, all of my property, real, personal, and mixed, of whatever kind and wherever situated, of which I may die possessed, to my spouse, (3)_____, if my spouse survives me.

B. If my spouse does not survive me, I leave my residuary estate to the following: (4)

    1. _____
       _____

    2. _____
       _____

    3. _____
       _____
       _____
       _____

3. Appointment of Fiduciaries

A. Executor. I appoint my spouse to serve as my executor. If my spouse cannot serve, then I appoint (5)_____ to serve as my executor.

B. Trustee. I appoint (6)_____ to serve as my trustee. If (6)_____ cannot serve, then I appoint (7)_____ to serve as my trustee.

C. No bond shall be required of my executor, or trustee.

Initials: (11)_____ (12)_____ _____ _____   Page _____ of _____
           Testator   Witness   Witness   Witness

Married without Children

4. Young Person's Trust

My trustee shall hold the assets passing to young persons in a separate trust for each young person under this article until that young person has reached the age of (8)_____ years, the termination date.

    A. Until the termination date, my trustee shall distribute to or for the benefit of the young person as much of the net income and principal as my trustee may consider appropriate for the young person's health, education, support, or maintenance, annually adding to principal any undistributed income.

    B. Upon the termination date, my trustee shall distribute the remaining assets to the young person.

5. Miscellaneous

My executor shall exercise all powers conferred by law, in addition to the following powers, which are to be exercised in the best interest of my estate or trust.

    A. To hold and retain any property owned by me.

    B. To sell, exchange, or lease any property.

    C. To vote stock; to convert securities belonging to my estate into other securities; and, to exercise all other rights and privileges of a person owning similar properties.

    D. To settle claims.

    E. To pay all debts and taxes.

    F. To do all other acts necessary for the proper management, investment, and distribution of my estate or trust.

    G. To take all actions to have the probate of this Will conducted as free of court supervision as possible.

I have signed this Will in the presence of the undersigned witnesses on this (9)_____ day of _____, 20_____, at (10)_____, State of _____, and declare it is my Will, that I signed it willingly, that I executed it as my free and voluntary act for the purpose expressed herein, and that I am of legal age and sound mind.

[Do Not Sign]_____
[Signature]

[Signatures of witnesses not provided.]

Unmarried with Adult Children (Will Form 4)

Unmarried means without a spouse no matter what the reason—your choice, death of spouse, or divorce. Use this Will Form 4, *Unmarried with Adult Children*, if you are unmarried, all of your children are adults, and you wish the following to happen upon your death.

❏ Your adult children (including adopted children) inherit your estate in equal shares.

❏ If one or more of your children dies before you do, that child's children (your grandchildren) inherit your dead child's portion, in equal shares.

❏ If your dead child has no living children, your living children inherit the dead child's portion, in equal shares.

❏ If any grandchildren inherit your estate because of a dead child, and the grandchildren are young, the portion of your estate your grandchildren inherit is held in trust until they reach an age you select.

❏ You select an executor and an alternate executor.

❏ You select a trustee and an alternate trustee for your Grandchild's Trust.

❏ You waive the requirement that your executor and trustee post a bond.

❏ You give your executor and trustee the authority to wind up your financial affairs, including the distribution of your property to your beneficiaries.

An Example of Unmarried with Adult Children

Now look at the sample, filled-in form on page 45 to see how the *Unmarried with Adult Children* Will form works. It is based on the following situation.

John Smith is widowed. He has two children, David (26) and Ann (24). David, an investment banker, is married and has three children—Sarah (8), Susie (6), and Ricky (4). Ann, a nurse, has one child—Katherine (2). John wants his children to inherit equal 50% shares of his property. If David predeceases him, John wants David's three children to split equally the 50% share of his estate that David would have inherited if David had outlived him. If Ann predeceases him, John wants Ann's child to inherit the 50% share of his estate that Ann would have inherited if Ann had outlived him. If any of his grandchildren inherit from him because of the death of a parent, John wants the grandchild's share of his estate kept in trust until the grandchild reaches the age of 21 (Grandchild's Trust). John wants David to be executor, with Ann as alternate. John wants his surviving child to be trustee of the Grandchild's Trust, so he names David as trustee, with Ann as alternate trustee.

SAMPLE, FILLED-IN WILL FORM 4
Unmarried with Adult Children

Will of _____ John Smith _____

I, _____ John Smith _____ of _____ Any Town, Any State _____,
make this my Will. I revoke any other Wills and codicils made by me.

1. Family

I have ___2___ children, _____ David Smith and Ann Jones _____, my children.
The term "my children" includes the aforementioned children and all children born after the making of this will and all children adopted by me.

2. Residuary Estate

A. I give my residuary estate, that is, all of my property, real, personal, and mixed, of whatever kind and wherever situated, of which I may die possessed, in equal shares, to my children.

B. If a child does not survive me, then the deceased child's share devolves, in equal shares, to the deceased child's children. If none of the deceased child's children survive me, then this share devolves, in equal shares, to my surviving children.

C. If a deceased child's children are entitled to a share of my estate, I leave this bequest to my trustee to be held in trust under Article 4, "Grandchildren's Trust."

3. Appointment of Fiduciaries

A. Executor. I appoint _____ David Smith _____ to serve as my executor. If _____ David Smith _____ cannot serve, then I appoint _____ Ann Jones _____ to serve as my executor.

B. Trustee. I appoint _____ David Smith _____ to serve as my trustee. If _____ David Smith _____ cannot serve, then I appoint _____ Ann Jones _____ to serve as my trustee.

C. No bond shall be required of my executor or trustee.

Unmarried with Adult Children

4. Grandchild's Trust

My trustee shall hold the assets passing to my grandchildren in a separate trust for each grandchild under this article until that grandchild has reached the age of __21__ years, the termination date.

    A. Until the termination date, my trustee shall distribute to or for the benefit of my grandchild as much of the net income and principal as my trustee may consider appropriate for the grandchild's health, education, support, or maintenance, annually adding to principal any undistributed income.

    B. Upon the termination date, my trustee shall distribute the remaining assets to the grandchild.

5. Miscellaneous

My executor and trustee shall exercise all powers conferred by law, in addition to the following powers, which are to be exercised in the best interest of my estate or trust.

    A. To hold and retain any property owned by me.

    B. To sell, exchange, or lease any property.

    C. To vote stock; to convert securities belonging to my estate into other securities; and, to exercise all other rights and privileges of a person owning similar properties.

    D. To settle claims.

    E. To pay all debts and taxes.

    F. To do all other acts necessary for the proper management, investment, and distribution of my estate or trust.

    G. To take all actions to have the probate of this Will conducted as free of court supervision as possible.

I have signed this Will in the presence of the undersigned witnesses on this __18th__ day of _____January_____, 20__06__, at _____Any Town_____, State of _____Any State_____, and declare it is my Will, that I signed it willingly, that I executed it as my free and voluntary act for the purpose expressed herein, and that I am of legal age and sound mind.

_John Smith_____
[Signature]

[Signatures of witnesses not provided.]

Continuing the Conversation about Will Form 4

Client:

I just want to make sure I understand the legalese. The children inherit everything I own in equal shares, correct?

Lawyer:

Yes. Article 2.A makes this clear.

> Article 2.A. I give my residuary estate, that is, all of my property, real, personal, and mixed, of whatever kind and wherever situated, of which I may die possessed, in equal shares, to my children.

Client:

And my grandchildren do not inherit anything from me if all of my children are alive at my death?

Lawyer:

Correct. The only time a grandchild would inherit from you would be if your child (their parent) died before you. The dead child's share would be split equally between that dead child's children. For example, if David died, his 50% share would be split equally between his three children. If Ann died, her 50% share would be given to her only child. If David and Ann both outlived John, they would each inherit 50% of his estate.

Client:

Which of my grown children should I name my executor?

Lawyer:

People often wrestle with this question. It is best to appoint just one of your children as executor. It saves a lot of paperwork. If you have two executors, you have to get two signatures on checks, court papers, and so on. It's administratively easier with a single executor. Some parents name the child who lives the closest to them, thinking the duties of executor would be less burdensome on the geographically close child. Some parents make their decision based on which child is better with finances, since executor's duties are primarily financial. John chose his investment banker son to be executor and his nurse daughter as alternate. If you are concerned with family harmony, you might consider discussing your decision, and the reasons for it, with all of your children while you can.

Client:
Who should I make trustee? I want to keep this job in the family.

Lawyer:
The Grandchild's Trust only comes into existence if one of your children die before you. The trustee's job is to manage the money going to your underage grandchild. The trustee obviously will have nothing to do with the custody of the grandchild. I recommend picking the child you think is the best money manager as primary trustee and the child who is the next best money manager, as the alternate trustee. John chose his investment bank son to be primary trustee and his nurse daughter as alternate trustee.

Client:
What does the grandchild's trustee have to do?

Lawyer:
The grandchild's trustee has to manage the money in the trust until the grandchild reaches the age you select. John Smith selected 21 years of age. If Ann was dead at John's death, David would be trustee for Ann's daughter's (Katherine) 50% share of John's estate. David, as the trustee, would invest the trust funds and decide the amount of trust funds to be given to Katherine's guardian (probably her father) for Katherine's benefit. Trust funds could be used for health, education, support, and maintenance expenses. When Katherine turns 21, David would have to give her any money remaining in the trust fund.

Instructions for Completing the Draft Will Form 4—Unmarried with Adult Children

Gather the following information:

1. Your name.
2. Your city and state.
3. The number of children you have.
4. Your child or children's name(s).
5. Your executor's name. You will fill in this name in the blanks of the draft two times.
6. Your alternate executor's name.
7. Your trustee's name. You will fill in this name in the blanks of the draft two times.
8. Your alternate trustee's name.
9. The age at which your grandchildren must receive their inheritances.
10. The date you will sign your Will.
11. The city and state where you sign your Will.
12. Your initials.
13. Your witnesses' initials.

Now you are ready to fill in your draft form. Fill in your information next to the numbered blank in the draft. Your draft is the place for you to experiment, and to make and correct errors. You do not want erasures on your Will. It may be a good idea to live with the draft of the Will for a few days before filling out your final Will. Do not sign the draft. When you are ready, continue on to Chapter 3 to create your Self-Proving Affidavit, and then on to Chapter 6, which contains instructions for preparing and signing your Will. Do not forget to prepare your Living Will (Chapter 4) and Power of Attorney (Chapter 5). It is easy to complete these two documents while you have the witnesses and notary present for the signing of your Will.

Unmarried with Adult Children

Draft
Unmarried with Adult Children

Will of (1)_____

I, (1)_____ of (2)_____,
make this my Will. I revoke any other Wills and codicils made by me.

1. Family

I have (3)_____ children, (4)_____, my
children. The term "my children" includes the aforementioned children and all children born after
the making of this will and all children adopted by me.

2. Residuary Estate

A. I give my residuary estate, that is, all of my property, real, personal, and mixed, of whatever
   kind and wherever situated, of which I may die possessed, in equal shares, to my children.

B. If a child does not survive me, then the deceased child's share devolves, in equal shares,
   to the deceased child's children. If none of the deceased child's children survive me, then
   this share devolves, in equal shares, to my surviving children.

C. If a deceased child's children are entitled to a share of my estate, I leave this bequest to
   my trustee to be held in trust under Article 4, "Grandchildren's Trust."

3. Appointment of Fiduciaries

A. Executor. I appoint (5)_____ to serve as my executor. If
   (5)_____ cannot serve, then I appoint (6)_____
   to serve as my executor.

B. Trustee. I appoint (7)_____ to serve as my trustee. If
   (7)_____ cannot serve, then I appoint (8)_____
   to serve as my trustee.

C. No bond shall be required of my executor or trustee.

4. Grandchild's Trust

My trustee shall hold the assets passing to my grandchildren in a separate trust for each grandchild under this article until that grandchild has reached the age of (9)_____ years, the termination date.

    A. Until the termination date, my trustee shall distribute to or for the benefit of my grandchild as much of the net income and principal as my trustee may consider appropriate for the grandchild's health, education, support, or maintenance, annually adding to principal any undistributed income.

    B. Upon the termination date, my trustee shall distribute the remaining assets to the grandchild.

5. Miscellaneous

My executor and trustee shall exercise all powers conferred by law, in addition to the following powers, which are to be exercised in the best interest of my estate or trust.

    A. To hold and retain any property owned by me.

    B. To sell, exchange, or lease any property.

    C. To vote stock; to convert securities belonging to my estate into other securities; and, to exercise all other rights and privileges of a person owning similar properties.

    D. To settle claims.

    E. To pay all debts and taxes.

    F. To do all other acts necessary for the proper management, investment, and distribution of my estate or trust.

    G. To take all actions to have the probate of this Will conducted as free of court supervision as possible.

I have signed this Will in the presence of the undersigned witnesses on this (10)_____ day of _____, 20_____, at (11)_____, State of (11)_____, and declare it is my Will, that I signed it willingly, that I executed it as my free and voluntary act for the purpose expressed herein, and that I am of legal age and sound mind.

[Do Not Sign]_____
[Signature]

[Signatures of witnesses not provided.]

Unmarried with Adult Children

Initials: (12)_____ (13)_____ _____ _____
          Testator   Witness   Witness   Witness

Unmarried with Young Children (Will Form 5)

Use Will Form 5, *Unmarried with Young Children*, if you are unmarried and any of your children are young. Even if you have adult children (with possible young children of their own), you still use this form if any of your children are young. *Unmarried* means without a spouse, no matter what the reason—choice, death of a spouse, or a divorce. This form keeps all of your property in trust, for the benefit of all of your children, until your youngest child reaches an age you select. Use this form if you wish the following to happen upon your death.

❏ If one or more of your children are young at your death, all of your estate will be held in a Children's Trust until your youngest child reaches the age you select (usually 21). Money from this trust can be spent on all of your children during the life of the trust. The trust ends when your youngest child reaches the age you select. When it ends, any property in the trust is distributed equally to all of your children.

❏ If one or more of your children is dead at your death, leaving children, that dead child's children (your grandchildren) inherit your dead child's portion, in equal shares.

❏ If your dead child has no living children, your living children inherit the dead child's portion, in equal shares.

❏ If any grandchildren inherit your estate because of a dead child, and the grandchildren are young, the portion of your estate your grandchildren inherit is held in trust until they reach the age you specify (Grandchild's Trust).

❏ You select an executor and an alternate executor.

❏ You select a guardian and an alternate guardian to care for minor children.

❏ You select a trustee and an alternate trustee for the Children's and Grandchild's Trust.

❏ You waive the requirement that your executor and trustee post a bond.

❏ You give your executor and trustee the authority to wind up your financial affairs, including the distribution of your property to your beneficiaries.

An Example of Unmarried with Young Children

The sample, filled-in form on page 54 shows how the *Unmarried with Young Children* Will form works. It is based on the following situation.

John Smith is widowed. He has two children, David (18) and Ann (12). If John dies before Ann reaches age 21, he wants all of his property held in trust for the benefit of both children until Ann reaches 21, when the money is given outright, in equal shares, to both children. If a child dies during the course of this trust, the surviving child will be given all of the money. If Ann is 21 at John's death, he wants his children to inherit equal 50% shares of his property, outright and free of trust. If a child dies leaving children, John wants the dead child's children to inherit equal shares of the dead child's portion of his estate. If a grandchild inherits because of the death of his child, John wants the grandchild's share of his estate kept in trust until the grandchild reaches the age of 21 (Grandchild's Trust). John wants his accountant brother, Harry Smith, to be his executor and trustee. John wants his deceased wife's sister, Nancy Evans, to be guardian with custody of his minor children and alternate trustee. If Nancy cannot be guardian, he wants Harry to be guardian. If Harry cannot be trustee, he wants Nancy to be trustee.

SAMPLE, FILLED-IN WILL FORM 5
Unmarried with Young Children

Will of _____ John Smith _____

I, _____ John Smith _____ of _____ Any Town, Any State _____,
make this my Will. I revoke any other Wills and codicils made by me.

1. Family

I have __2__ children, _____ David Smith and Ann Smith _____, my children.
The term "my children" includes the aforementioned children and all children born after the making of this will and all children adopted by me.

2. Residuary Estate

A. I give my residuary estate, that is, all of my property, real, personal, and mixed, of whatever kind and wherever situated, of which I may die possessed, to my children. If my youngest child has, on the date of my death, reached the age of __21__ years, I leave this residuary estate outright, in equal shares, to my children. If my youngest child has not, on the date of my death, reached the age of __21__ years, I leave this residuary estate to my trustee to be held in trust under Article 4, "Children's Trust."

B. If a child does not survive me and no "Children's Trust" is created according to Article 2.A above, then the deceased child's share devolves, in equal shares, to the deceased child's children. If none of the deceased child's children survive me, then this share devolves, in equal shares, to my surviving children.

C. If a deceased child's children are entitled to a share of my estate, I leave this bequest to my trustee to be held in trust under Article 5, "Grandchild's Trust."

3. Appointment of Fiduciaries

A. Executor. I appoint _____ Harry Smith _____ to serve as my executor. If _____ Harry Smith _____ cannot serve, then I appoint _____ Nancy Evans _____ to serve as my executor.

B. Guardian. If, at my death, any of my children are minors, and a guardian is needed for my minor children, I appoint _____ Nancy Evans _____ to serve as my guardian. If _____ Nancy Evans _____ cannot serve, then I appoint _____ Harry Smith _____ to serve as my guardian.

C. Trustee. I appoint _____ **Harry Smith** _____ to serve as my trustee. If _____ **Harry Smith** _____ cannot serve, then I appoint _____ **Nancy Evans** _____ to serve as my trustee.

D. No bond shall be required of my executor, trustee, or guardian.

4. Children's Trust

If a "Children's Trust" is created according to Article 2.A above, my trustee shall hold the assets passing to my children in trust under this article.

A. Until the termination date, my trustee shall distribute to or for the benefit of my children as much of the net income and principal as my trustee may consider appropriate for their health, education, support, or maintenance, annually adding to principal any undistributed income. My trustee may distribute income and principal unequally and may distribute to some children and not to others. My trustee may consider other income and assets readily available to my children in making distributions.

B. Upon the termination date, my trustee shall distribute the remaining assets, in equal shares, to my surviving children.

C. The termination date is the date on which my youngest living child has reached the age of __21__ years.

5. Grandchild's Trust

My trustee shall hold the assets passing to my grandchildren in a separate trust for each grandchild under this article until that grandchild has reached the age of __21__ years, the termination date.

A. Until the termination date, my trustee shall distribute to or for the benefit of my grandchild as much of the net income and principal as my trustee may consider appropriate for the grandchild's health, education, support, or maintenance, annually adding to principal any undistributed income.

B. Upon the termination date, my trustee shall distribute the remaining assets to the grandchild.

6. Miscellaneous

My executor and trustee shall exercise all powers conferred by law, in addition to the following powers, which are to be exercised in the best interest of my estate or trust.

A. To hold and retain any property owned by me.

B. To sell, exchange, or lease any property.

C. To vote stock; to convert securities belonging to my estate into other securities; and, to exercise all other rights and privileges of a person owning similar properties.

Unmarried with Young Children

D. To settle claims.

E. To pay all debts and taxes.

F. To do all other acts necessary for the proper management, investment, and distribution of my estate or trust.

G. To take all actions to have the probate of this Will conducted as free of court supervision as possible.

I have signed this Will in the presence of the undersigned witnesses on this __18th__ day of _____January_____, 20_06_, at _____Any Town_____, State of _____Any State_____, and declare it is my Will, that I signed it willingly, that I executed it as my free and voluntary act for the purpose expressed herein, and that I am of legal age and sound mind.

John Smith
[Signature]

[Signatures of witnesses not provided.]

Unmarried with Young Children

Continuing the Conversation about Will Form 5

Client:

I want to make sure I understand when to use this form. If I have adult children and young children, I use the Unmarried with Young Children form?

Lawyer:

Correct. If you have a 25-year-old son and a 15-year-old son, use this form. It keeps all your money in trust until your fifteen year-old son reaches the age you select. At your death, if all your children have reached the age you have selected, no Children's Trust will be established. If one child dies before you, that child's children will inherit the deceased parent's share of your estate.

Client:

I just want to make sure I understand the legalese. My children inherit everything I own. If I die when a child is under an age I select, all of my property goes into a Children's Trust. If my children are both over an age I select at my death, all of my property is inherited, in equal shares, by my children.

Lawyer:

Correct. Article 2.A makes this clear.

> Article 2.A. I give my residuary estate, that is, all of my property, real, personal, and mixed, of whatever kind and wherever situated, of which I may die possessed, to my children. If my youngest child has, on the date of my death, reached the age of 21 years, I leave this residuary estate outright, in equal shares, to my children. If my youngest child has not, on the date of my death, reached the age of 21 years, I leave this residuary estate to my trustee to be held in trust under Article 4, "Children's Trust."

Unmarried with Young Children

Client:
Can you explain the Children's Trust?

Lawyer:
If one of your children is under an age you select (usually 21), everything you own goes into a Children's Trust. If John dies when daughter Ann is 12 and son David is 18, all of John's property goes into a Children's Trust, managed by brother Harry for nine years, until Ann turns 21. Trustee Harry can spend trust funds on both Ann and David during these nine years and does not have to spend equal amounts on each child. The Children's Trust allows the trustee the same flexibility that the parent has to spend more on one child, as circumstances dictate, than another child. In my experience, it is better for the parent not to try to rule from the grave. Unexpected things happen. One child may have greater medical or educational expenses than another. You should make sure that your trustee understands your wishes for your children. When Ann turns 21, she and David are entitled to split equally whatever remains of the trust fund. So equality per child principle is maintained, after both children have reached age 21.

NOTE: *If a child dies in the course of this trust and has children, your surviving child—not your grandchildren—inherit the dead child's portion of the Children's Trust.*

Client:
So my grandchildren do not inherit anything from me if all of my children are alive at my death?

Lawyer:
Correct. The only time a grandchild would inherit from you is if your child, their parent, died before you and no Children's Trust was established. The dead child's share would be split equally between that dead child's children. For example, if David died, his 50% share would be split equally between his children. If Ann died, her 50% share would be split equally between his children. If David and Ann both outlived John, they would each inherit 50% of his estate.

Client:
What does the trustee of the Grandchild's Trust have to do?

Lawyer:
The grandchild's trustee has to manage the money in your Grandchild's Trust until the grandchild reaches an age your select. John selected the age of 21, at which time the trustee must give the grandchild any money remaining in the Grandchild's Trust.

Client:
My children are young now. Why am I worrying about a Grandchild's Trust?

Lawyer:
Your Will governs circumstances present when you die, not when you make it. Hopefully, John will still be alive in forty years, when his children are 52 and 58, with teenagers of their own. If David dies before John, and has his own children, John wants David's children to inherit equally David's share. But the grandchildren would not inherit until they reached age 21. Their share would be kept in trust—a Grandchild's Trust.

Client:
What does the trustee of the Children's Trust have to do?

Lawyer:
The trustee manages the trust funds for the life of the trust. The trustee also has the discretion to decide how much of the trust funds should be spent on which child. Trust funds can be spent on health, education, maintenance, and support expenses of the children. But the trustee does not have personal custody and control over your children. That responsibility falls to their guardian. Trustee Harry and the Guardian Nancy would confer on the needs of the children, and Harry would give Guardian Nancy money to spend on the children.

Client:
What does the guardian do?

Lawyer:
The guardian has custody of your children until they reach legal majority, which is 18 years of age in most states. The person you name as guardian of your children must, in most states, also be appointed by the courts. The judge pays attention to the parent's wishes as to guardian. The parent's Will is the place the judge looks to find out the parent's wishes. The judge considers the best interest of the child in making the guardian appointment.

Client:
Under the Children's Trust, my oldest child would not get money from my estate until my youngest child reached an age I select. Correct?

Lawyer:
Correct. All of your property is held in trust until your youngest child reaches an age your select. But remember, an older child can receive money from the trustee. It's just that the older child has no right to receive any money directly from the trust until the youngest reaches the age you select.

Instructions for Completing the Draft Will Form 5—Unmarried with Young Children

Gather the following information:

1. Your name.
2. Your city and state.
3. The number of children you have.
4. Your child or children's name(s). (Add more lines if you have more than two children.)
5. The age that your youngest child must reach in order for all your children to receive their inheritance outright (without a trust). You will fill in this number in the blanks of the draft three times.
6. Your executor's name. You will fill in this name in the blanks of the draft two times.
7. Your alternate executor's name.
8. Your guardian's name. You will fill in this name in the blanks of the draft two times.
9. Your alternate guardian's name.
10. Your trustee's name. You will fill in this name in the blanks of the draft two times.
11. Your alternate trustee's name.
12. The age at which any grandchild must receive his or her inheritance.
13. The date you will sign your Will.
14. The city and state where you sign your Will.
15. Your initials.
16. Your witnesses' initials.

Now you are ready to fill in your draft form. Fill in your information next to the numbered blank in the draft. Your draft is the place for you to experiment, and to make and correct errors. You do not want erasures on your Will. It may be a good idea to live with the draft of your Will for a few days before filling out your final Will. Do not sign the draft. When you are ready, continue on to Chapter 3 to create your Self-Proving Affidavit, and then on to Chapter 6, which contains instructions for preparing and signing your Will. Do not forget to prepare your Living Will (Chapter 4) and Power of Attorney (Chapter 5). It is easy to complete these two documents while you have the witnesses and notary present for the signing of your Will.

Draft
Unmarried with Young Children

Will of (1)_____

I, (1)_____ of (2)_____,
make this my Will. I revoke any other Wills and codicils made by me.

1. Family

I have (3)_____ children, (4)_____, my
children. The term "my children" includes the aforementioned children and all children born after
the making of this will and all children adopted by me.

2. Residuary Estate

A. I give my residuary estate, that is, all of my property, real, personal, and mixed, of whatever kind and wherever situated, of which I may die possessed, to my children. If my
   youngest child has, on the date of my death, reached the age of (5)_____ years, I leave
   this residuary estate outright, in equal shares, to my children. If my youngest child has
   not, on the date of my death, reached the age of (5)_____ years, I leave this residuary
   estate to my trustee to be held in trust under Article 4, "Children's Trust."

B. If a child does not survive me and no "Children's Trust" is created according to Article
   2.A above, then the deceased child's share devolves, in equal shares, to the deceased
   child's children. If none of the deceased child's children survive me, then this share
   devolves, in equal shares, to my surviving children.

C. If a deceased child's children are entitled to a share of my estate, I leave this bequest to
   my trustee to be held in trust under Article 5, "Grandchild's Trust."

3. Appointment of Fiduciaries

A. Executor. I appoint (6)_____ to serve as my executor. If
   (6)_____ cannot serve, then I appoint (7)_____
   to serve as my executor.

B. Guardian. If, at my death, any of my children are minors, and a guardian is needed for
   my minor children, I appoint (8)_____to serve as my guardian.
   If (8)_____ cannot serve, then I appoint (9)_____
   to serve as my guardian.

Initials: (15)_____ (16)_____ _____ _____   Page _____ of _____
            Testator   Witness   Witness   Witness

C. Trustee. I appoint (10)_____ to serve as my trustee. If (10)_____ cannot serve, then I appoint (11)_____ to serve as my trustee.

D. No bond shall be required of my executor, trustee, or guardian.

4. Children's Trust

If a "Children's Trust" is created according to Article 2.A above, my trustee shall hold the assets passing to my children in trust under this article.

A. Until the termination date, my trustee shall distribute to or for the benefit of my children as much of the net income and principal as my trustee may consider appropriate for their health, education, support, or maintenance, annually adding to principal any undistributed income. My trustee may distribute income and principal unequally and may distribute to some children and not to others. My trustee may consider other income and assets readily available to my children in making distributions.

B. Upon the termination date, my trustee shall distribute the remaining assets, in equal shares, to my surviving children.

C. The termination date is the date on which my youngest living child has reached the age of (5)_____ years.

5. Grandchild's Trust

My trustee shall hold the assets passing to my grandchildren in a separate trust for each grandchild under this article until that grandchild has reached the age of (12)_____ years, the termination date.

A. Until the termination date, my trustee shall distribute to or for the benefit of my grandchild as much of the net income and principal as my trustee may consider appropriate for the grandchild's health, education, support, or maintenance, annually adding to principal any undistributed income.

B. Upon the termination date, my trustee shall distribute the remaining assets to the grandchild.

6. Miscellaneous

My executor and trustee shall exercise all powers conferred by law, in addition to the following powers, which are to be exercised in the best interest of my estate or trust.

A. To hold and retain any property owned by me.

B. To sell, exchange, or lease any property.

C. To vote stock; to convert securities belonging to my estate into other securities; and, to exercise all other rights and privileges of a person owning similar properties.

Unmarried with Young Children

D. To settle claims.

E. To pay all debts and taxes.

F. To do all other acts necessary for the proper management, investment, and distribution of my estate or trust.

G. To take all actions to have the probate of this Will conducted as free of court supervision as possible.

I have signed this Will in the presence of the undersigned witnesses on this (13)_____ day of _____, 20_____, at (14)_____, State of (14)_____, and declare it is my Will, that I signed it willingly, that I executed it as my free and voluntary act for the purpose expressed herein, and that I am of legal age and sound mind.

[Do Not Sign] _____

[Signature]

[Signatures of witnesses not provided.]

Unmarried without Children (Will Form 6)

Use Will Form 6, *Unmarried without Children,* if you are unmarried without children and you wish the following to happen upon your death. (*Unmarried* can mean by choice, widowed, or divorced.)

❏ Your property goes to whomever you name in your Will.

❏ If any of your beneficiaries are young, your gift is held in trust until they reach an age you select (Young Person's Trust).

❏ You select an executor and alternate executor.

❏ You select a trustee and alternate trustee for the Young Person's Trust.

❏ You waive the requirement that your executor and trustee post a bond.

❏ You give your executor and trustee the authority to wind up your financial affairs, including the distribution of your property to your beneficiaries.

An Example of Unmarried without Children

The sample, filled-in form on page 66 shows how the *Unmarried without Children* Will form works. It is based on the following situation.

John Smith is unmarried and has no children. John wants his brother, Paul Smith, to inherit half of his property, and his deceased wife Mary's two sisters, Sally Davis and Nancy Evans, to each inherit a 25% portion of his property. Paul and Sally both have children. Nancy has no children. If Paul or Sally should die before him, John wants their children to inherit the share that their parent would have inherited. If Nancy dies before him, he wants Sally, or her children, to inherit Nancy's share. If any beneficiary is under age 21, John wants the young person's share of his estate to be held in trust until the young person reaches the age of 21. John wants his brother, Paul, to be his executor and trustee of the Young Person's Trust. If Paul cannot be executor and trustee, he wants Nancy to be executor and trustee.

SAMPLE, FILLED-IN WILL FORM 6
Unmarried without Children

Will of _____ John Smith _____

I, _____ John Smith _____ of _____ Any Town, Any State _____,
make this my Will. I revoke any other Wills and codicils made by me.

1. Residuary Estate

A. I give my residuary estate, that is, all of my property, real, personal, and mixed, of whatever kind and wherever situated, of which I may die possessed to:

1. 50% to my brother, Paul Smith, if he survives me. If he does not survive me, this bequest is given to his children who survive me, in equal shares.

2. 25% to Sally Davis, if she survives me. If she does not survive me, this bequest is given to her children who survive me, in equal shares.

3. 25% to Nancy Evans, if she survives me. If she does not survive me, this bequest is given to Sally Davis, if she survives me. If Sally Davis does not survive me, this bequest is given to the children of Sally Davis who survive me, in equal shares.

2. Appointment of Fiduciaries

A. Executor. I appoint _____ Paul Smith _____ to serve as my executor. If _____ Paul Smith _____ cannot serve, then I appoint _____ Sally Davis _____ to serve as my executor.

B. Trustee. I appoint _____ Paul Smith _____ to serve as my trustee. If _____ Paul Smith _____ cannot serve, then I appoint _____ Sally Davis _____ to serve as my trustee.

C. No bond shall be required of my executor or trustee.

3. Young Person's Trust

My trustee shall hold the assets passing to young persons in a trust for each young person under this article until that young person has reached the age of _21_ years, the termination date.

A. Until the termination date, my trustee shall distribute to or for the benefit of the young person as much of the net income and principal as my trustee may consider appropriate

for the young person's health, education, support, or maintenance, annually adding to principal any undistributed income.
B. Upon the termination date, my trustee shall distribute the remaining assets to the young person.

4. Miscellaneous

My executor shall exercise all powers conferred by law, in addition to the following powers, which are to be exercised in the best interest of my estate or trust.
A. To hold and retain any property owned by me.
B. To sell, exchange, or lease any property.
C. To vote stock; to convert securities belonging to my estate into other securities; and, to exercise all other rights and privileges of a person owning similar properties.
D. To settle claims.
E. To pay all debts and taxes.
F. To do all other acts necessary for the proper management, investment, and distribution of my estate or trust.
G. To take all actions to have the probate of this Will conducted as free of court supervision as possible.

I have signed this Will in the presence of the undersigned witnesses on this __18th__ day of _____January_____, 20__06__, at _____Any Town_____, State of _____Any State_____, and declare it is my Will, that I signed it willingly, that I executed it as my free and voluntary act for the purpose expressed herein, and that I am of legal age and sound mind.

John Smith
_____
[Signature]

[Signatures of witnesses not provided.]

Unmarried without Children

Initials: __*JS*__ __*W1*__ __*W2*__ __*W3*__   Page __2__ of __2__
Testator   Witness   Witness   Witness

Continuing the Conversation about Will Form 6

Client:

What are important things to make sure of if I am unmarried and have no children?

Lawyer:

You need to remember that your Will isn't valid until you are dead. Make sure you specify who gets your property if the people you name in your Will are dead. The law has phrases that accomplish this if you have children. But if you don't have children, you need to specify whether your gift goes to the children of your beneficiary. If you do not want your gift to go to the children of your beneficiary, you must designate who gets the gift.

Client:

What does the trustee for the Young Person's Trust have to do?

Lawyer:

The young person's trustee has to manage the money in the Young Person's Trust until the young person reaches an age you select. John Smith selected 21 years of age. His trustee, Paul, would invest the trust funds and decide how much of the trust should be given to the young person for health, education, maintenance, and support expenses. When the young person reaches the age of 21, Paul would have to give the young person any money remaining in the trust fund.

Instructions for Completing the Draft Will Form 6—Unmarried without Children

Gather the following information:

1. Your name.
2. Your city and state.
3. A list of those who you wish to receive your estate. If you do not want these beneficiaries' children to receive your gift if your beneficiary predeceases you, then you must designate who you want to receive your gift.
4. Your executor's name. You will fill in this name in the blanks of the draft two times.
5. Your alternate executor's name.
6. Your trustee's name. You will fill in this name in the blanks of the draft two times.
7. Your alternate trustee's name.
8. The age at which young beneficiaries must receive their inheritance.
9. The date you will sign your Will.
10. The city and state where you sign your Will.
11. Your initials.
12. Your witnesses' initials.

Now you are ready to fill in your draft form. Fill in your information next to the numbered blank in the draft. Your draft is the place for you to experiment, to make and correct errors. You do not want erasures on your Will. It may be a good idea to live with the draft of your Will for a few days before filling out your final Will. Do not sign the draft. When you are ready, continue on to Chapter 3 to create your Self-Proving Affidavit and then on to Chapter 6, which contains instructions for preparing and signing your Will. Do not forget to prepare your Living Will (Chapter 4) and Power of Attorney (Chapter 5). It is easy to complete these two documents while you have the witnesses and notary present for the signing of your Will.

Unmarried without Children

Draft
Unmarried without Children

Will of (1)_____

I, (1)_____ of (2)_____,
make this my Will. I revoke any other Wills and codicils made by me.

1. Residuary Estate

A. I give my residuary estate, that is, all of my property, real, personal, and mixed, of whatever kind and wherever situated, of which I may die possessed to: (3)

1. _____
_____

2. _____
_____

3. _____
_____
_____
_____

2. Appointment of Fiduciaries

A. Executor. I appoint (4)_____ to serve as my executor. If
(4)_____ cannot serve, then I appoint (5)_____
to serve as my executor.

B. Trustee. I appoint (6)_____ to serve as my trustee. If
(6)_____ cannot serve, then I appoint (7)_____
to serve as my trustee.

C. No bond shall be required of my executor or trustee.

3. Young Person's Trust

My trustee shall hold the assets passing to young persons in a trust for each young person under this
article until that young person has reached the age of (8)_____ years, the termination date.

A. Until the termination date, my trustee shall distribute to or for the benefit of the young
person as much of the net income and principal as my trustee may consider appropriate

for the young person's health, education, support, or maintenance, annually adding to principal any undistributed income.

B. Upon the termination date, my trustee shall distribute the remaining assets to the young person.

4. Miscellaneous

My executor shall exercise all powers conferred by law, in addition to the following powers, which are to be exercised in the best interest of my estate or trust.

A. To hold and retain any property owned by me.

B. To sell, exchange, or lease any property.

C. To vote stock; to convert securities belonging to my estate into other securities; and, to exercise all other rights and privileges of a person owning similar properties.

D. To settle claims.

E. To pay all debts and taxes.

F. To do all other acts necessary for the proper management, investment, and distribution of my estate or trust.

G. To take all actions to have the probate of this Will conducted as free of court supervision as possible.

I have signed this Will in the presence of the undersigned witnesses on this (9)_____ day of _____, 20_____, at (10)_____, State of _____, and declare it is my Will, that I signed it willingly, that I executed it as my free and voluntary act for the purpose expressed herein, and that I am of legal age and sound mind.

[Do Not Sign]_____
[Signature]

[Signatures of witnesses not provided.]

Unmarried without Children

Witness Signatures

If you turn to the blank Will forms in the Appendix you will notice that each ends with the following statement.

> The foregoing instrument was on said date subscribed at the end thereof by _____, the above named testator who signed, published, and declared this instrument to be his/her Last Will and Testament in the presence of us and each of us, who thereupon at his/her request, in his/her presence, and in the presence of each other, have hereunto subscribed our names as witnesses thereto. We are of sound mind and proper age to witness a will and understand this to be his/her will, and to the best of our knowledge testator is of legal age to make a will, of sound mind, and under no constraint or undue influence.
>
> _____ residing at _____
> _____ residing at _____
> _____ residing at _____

This information will need to be completed with your name entered as testator, mark out either "his" or "her" depending on your gender, and the names and addresses of your witnesses. For our sample testator, John Smith, he would complete it as follows.

> The foregoing instrument was on said date subscribed at the end thereof by ___John Smith___, the above named testator who signed, published, and declared this instrument to be his/~~her~~ Last Will and Testament in the presence of us and each of us, who thereupon at his/~~her~~ request, in his/~~her~~ presence, and in the presence of each other, have hereunto subscribed our names as witnesses thereto. We are of sound mind and proper age to witness a will and understand this to be his/~~her~~ will, and to the best of our knowledge testator is of legal age to make a will, of sound mind, and under no constraint or undue influence.
>
> ___*Witness One*___ residing at 123 Main Street, Any Town, Any State
> ___*Witness Two*___ residing at 456 Oak Street, Any Town, Any State
> ___*Witness Three*___ residing at 789 Maple Drive, Any Town, Any State

Complete yours with the appropriate information. See page 128 for step-by-step instructions for executing your final Will and complete the witness signature information.

Chapter 3:
The Self-Proving Affidavit

A *Self-Proving Affidavit* is a simple document attached to your Will, in which a *notary public* essentially attests that your Will has been properly executed. It is a separate sheet of paper attached to the Will, signed by you and those who witnessed your Will, before being signed and sealed by the notary.

A Self-Proving Affidavit attached to your Will means that it can be immediately admitted to probate. This form represents an important step in determining that your Will is valid. It eliminates the requirement that the witnesses appear in court to swear that they did indeed witness your Will. Without this affidavit, time and money will be spent locating the witnesses and getting an affidavit from each of them.

Since your Will will not go into effect for many decades after you sign it, it might be difficult—if not impossible—to find your witnesses when you die. As you can see, it is certainly worth adding this brief form—properly signed, witnessed, and notarized—at the time you make your Will.

The list on page 74 tells you the appropriate Self-Proving Affidavit to use in your state. Forty-four states allow you to use either Self-Proving Affidavit Form A or Form B. Four states—California, the District of Columbia, Michigan, and Wisconsin—do not have a law that allows Self-Proving Affidavits to ease probate. And two states—Ohio and Vermont—do not make forms available. Residents of the six states that either have no law or form should still utilize the Self-Proving Affidavit, Form A. It does no harm to attach a Self-Proving Affidavit to your Will, and can make probate considerably easier if your state allows a Self-Proving Affidavit at the time your Will is being probated. These states are included on the listing under the first column for Form A.

You will note from the list that two states—New Hampshire and Texas—have unique Self-Proving Affidavits. They are completed in much the same manner as Form A, so you can use the instructions for Form A to complete these two documents (with the exception of designating your state, as this is printed on the form). The blank forms are included in the Appendix.

NOTE: *This book does not provide Wills for residents of Louisiana.*

Self-Proving Affidavit State List

FORM A

Alabama	Indiana	North Dakota
Alaska	Maine	Ohio
Arizona	Maryland	Oregon
Arkansas	Michigan	South Carolina
California	Minnesota	South Dakota
Colorado	Mississippi	Tennessee
Connecticut	Montana	Utah
District of Columbia	Nebraska	Vermont
Hawaii	Nevada	Washington
Idaho	New Mexico	West Virginia
Illinois	New York	Wisconsin

FORM B

Delaware	Kentucky	Oklahoma
Florida	Massachusetts	Pennsylvania
Georgia	Missouri	Rhode Island
Iowa	New Jersey	Virginia
Kansas	North Carolina	Wyoming

FORM C

New Hampshire

FORM D

Texas

Examples of Self-Proving Affidavits

Now look at four different sample, filled-in forms on pages 76 through 79 to see how the affidavit works. John Smith lives in Bethesda, Maryland, and needs Form A. His son, David Smith, lives in Alexandria, Virginia, and needs Form B. Susan Jones lives in Manchester, New Hampshire, and needs Form C. Mary Adams lives in Houston, Texas, and needs Form D.

SAMPLE, FILLED-IN FORM A

Self-Proving Affidavit

(attach to Will)

STATE OF _____Maryland_____

COUNTY OF _____Bethesda_____

We, _____John Smith_____, and _____First Witness_____, _____Second Witness_____, and _____Third Witness_____, the testator and the witnesses, whose names are signed to the attached or foregoing instrument in those capacities, personally appearing before the undersigned authority and being first duly sworn, declare to the undersigned authority under penalty of perjury that: 1) the testator declared, signed, and executed the instrument as his or her last Will; 2) he or she signed it willingly, or directed another to sign for him or her; 3) he or she executed it as his or her free and voluntary act for the purposes therein expressed; and 4) each of the witnesses, and the request of the testator, in his or her hearing and presence and in the presence of each other, signed the Will as witnesses, and that to the best of his or her knowledge the testator was at that time of full legal age, of sound mind, and under no constraint or undue influence.

_____*John Smith*_____ (Testator)

_____*First Witness*_____ (Witness)

_____*Second Witness*_____ (Witness)

_____*Third Witness*_____ (Witness)

Subscribed, sworn, and acknowledged before me, _____Any Notary_____, a notary public, and by _____John Smith_____, the testator, and by _____First Witness_____, _____Second Witness_____ and _____Third Witness_____, witnesses, this __18th__ day of _____December_____, 20__06__.

*Any Notary*_____

Notary Public

SAMPLE, FILLED-IN FORM B

Self-Proving Affidavit

(attach to Will)

STATE OF _____ Virginia _____

COUNTY OF _____ Alexandria _____

I, the undersigned, an officer authorized to administer oaths, certify that _____ David Smith _____,
the testator, and _____ First Witness _____, _____ Second Witness _____, and _____ Third Witness _____,
the witnesses, whose names are signed to the attached or foregoing instrument and whose signatures
appear below, having appeared before me and having been first been duly sworn, each then declared
to me that: 1) the attached or foregoing instrument is the last Will of the testator; 2) the testator willingly and voluntarily declared, signed, and executed the will in the presence of the witnesses; 3) the
witnesses signed the Will upon the request of the testator, in the presence and hearing of the testator and in the presence of each other; 4) to the best knowledge of each witness, the testator was, at
the time of signing, of the age of majority (or otherwise legally competent to make a Will), of sound
mind and memory, and under no constrain or undue influence; and, 5) each witness was and is
competent and of proper age to witness a Will.

_____ *David Smith* _____ (Testator)

_____ *First Witness* _____ (Witness)

_____ *Second Witness* _____ (Witness)

_____ *Third Witness* _____ (Witness)

Subscribed and sworn to before me by that _____ David Smith _____, the testator, who is personally known to me or who has produced a _____ driver's license _____ as identification, and by
_____ First Witness _____, a witness, who is personally known to me or who has produced a
_____ driver's license _____ as identification, and by _____ Second Witness _____, a witness, who is
personally known to me or who has produced a _____ driver's license _____ as identification, and
by _____ Third Witness _____ a witness, who is personally known to me or who has produced a
_____ driver's license _____ as identification, this __18th__ day of _____ December _____,
20 _06_ .

Any Notary _____

Notary or other officer

SAMPLE, FILLED-IN FORM C

Self-Proved Will Page—New Hampshire

(attach to Will)

STATE OF NEW HAMPSHIRE

COUNTY OF _____ Coos _____

The foregoing instrument was acknowledged before me this _____ January 18, 2006 _____ [day], by
_____ Susan Jones _____, the testator; _____ First Witness _____,
_____ Second Witness _____, and _____ Third Witness _____, the witnesses, who
under oath swear as follows:

1.   The testator signed the instrument as his Will or expressly directed another to sign for him.

2.   This was the testator's free and voluntary act for the purposes expressed in the Will.

3.   Each witness signed at the request of the testator, in his presence, and in the presence of the other witness.

4.   To the best of my knowledge, at the time of the signing the testator was at least 18 years of age, or if under 18 years was a married person, and was of sane mind and under no constraint or undue influence.

_____ *Any Notary* _____

Signature

_____ Any Notary _____

Official Capacity

SAMPLE, FILLED-IN FORM D

Self-Proved Will Affidavit—Texas

(attach to Will)

STATE OF TEXAS

COUNTY OF _____ Lubbock _____

Before me, the undersigned authority, on this day personally appeared _____ Mary Adams _____ _____ First Witness _____ , _____ Second Witness _____ , and _____ Third Witness _____ , known to me to be the testator and the witnesses, respectively, whose names are subscribed to the annexed or foregoing instrument in their respective capacities, and, all of said persons being by me duly sworn, the said _____ Mary Adams _____ testator, declared to me and to the said witnesses in my presence that said instrument is his or her last Will and testament, and that he or she had willingly made and executed it as his or her free act and deed, and the said witnesses, each on his or her oath stated to me in the presence and hearing of the said testator, that the said testator had declared to them that said instrument is his or her last Will and testament, and that he or she executed same as such and wanted each of them to sign it as a witness; and upon their oaths each witness stated further that they did sign the same as witnesses in the presence of the said testator and at his or her request; that he or she was at the time eighteen years of age or over (or being under such age, was or had been lawfully married, or was then a member of the armed forces of the United States or an auxiliary thereof or of the Maritime Service) and was of sound mind; and that each of said witnesses was then at least fourteen years of age.

_____ *Mary Adams* _____ (Testator)

_____ *First Witness* _____ (Witness)

_____ *Second Witness* _____ (Witness)

_____ *Third Witness* _____ (Witness)

Subscribed and sworn to before me by _____ John Smith _____, the testator, and by _____ First Witness _____ , _____ Second Witness _____ and _____ Third Witness _____ the witnesses, this __18th__ day of _____ January _____ , 20 __06__ .

Signed: _____ *Any Notary* _____

_____ Any Notary _____
Official Capacity of Officer

Instructions for Completing the Draft Form— Self-Proving Affidavit Form A

To complete the Self-Proving Affidavit, you must first select the form for your state from the Self-Proving Affidavit list on page 74. You will fill in your name next to all blank spaces containing number (3). At the signing of your Will and Self-Proving Affidavit, your witnesses and notary will fill in their names in the appropriate blanks as designated by the numbered instructions that follow.

1. The state where you live.
2. The county where you live.
3. Your name.
4. The names of your witnesses.
5. The name of the notary public.
6. The date you are signing the Self-Proving Affidavit.
7. The signature of the notary public.

Instructions for Completing the Draft Form— Self-Proving Affidavit Form B

To complete the Self-Proving Affidavit, you must first select the form for your state from the Self-Proving Affidavit list on page 74. You will fill in your name next to all blank spaces containing number (3). At the signing of your Will and Self-Proving Affidavit, your witnesses and notary will fill in their names in the appropriate blanks as designated by the numbered instructions that follow.

1. The state where you live.
2. The county where you live.
3. Your name.
4. The names of your witnesses.
5. The form of identification used (often a driver's license).
6. The date you are signing the Self-Proving Affidavit.
7. The signature of the notary public.

Instructions for Completing the Draft Form— Self-Proving Affidavit Form C (New Hampshire)

To complete the Self-Proving Affidavit, you must first select the form for your state from the Self-Proving Affidavit list on page 74. You will fill in your name next to all blank spaces containing number (2). At the signing of your Will and Self-Proving Affidavit, your witnesses and notary will fill in their names in the appropriate blanks as designated by the numbered instructions that follow.

1. The state where you live (already inserted on form).
2. The county where you live.
3. Your name.
4. The names of your witnesses.
5. The signature of the notary public.
6. The date you are signing the Self-Proving Affidavit.

Instructions for Completing the Draft Form— Self-Proving Affidavit Form D (Texas)

To complete the Self-Proving Affidavit, you must first select the form for your state from the Self-Proving Affidavit list on page 74. You will fill in your name next to all blank spaces containing number (2). At the signing of your Will and Self-Proving Affidavit, your witnesses and notary will fill in their names in the appropriate blanks as designated by the numbered instructions that follow.

1. The state where you live (already inserted on form).
2. The county where you live.
3. Your name.
4. The names of your witnesses.
5. The signature of the notary public.
6. The date you are signing the Self-Proving Affidavit.

Draft Form A

Self-Proving Affidavit

(attach to Will)

STATE OF (1)_____

COUNTY OF (2)_____

We, (3)_____, and (4)_____, (4)_____, and (4)_____, the testator and the witnesses, whose names are signed to the attached or foregoing instrument in those capacities, personally appearing before the undersigned authority and being first duly sworn, declare to the undersigned authority under penalty of perjury that: 1) the testator declared, signed, and executed the instrument as his or her last Will; 2) he or she signed it willingly, or directed another to sign for him or her; 3) he or she executed it as his or her free and voluntary act for the purposes therein expressed; and 4) each of the witnesses, and the request of the testator, in his or her hearing and presence and in the presence of each other, signed the Will as witnesses, and that to the best of his or her knowledge the testator was at that time of full legal age, of sound mind, and under no constraint or undue influence.

(3)_____[Do Not Sign]_____ (Testator)

(4)_____[Do Not Sign]_____ (Witness)

(4)_____[Do Not Sign]_____ (Witness)

(4)_____[Do Not Sign]_____ (Witness)

Subscribed, sworn, and acknowledged before me, (5)_____, a notary public, and by (3)_____, the testator, and by (4)_____, (4)_____ and (4)_____, witnesses, this (6)_____ day of _____, 20_____.

(7)_____[Do Not Sign]_____

Notary Public

Draft Form B

Self-Proving Affidavit
(attach to Will)

STATE OF (1)_____

COUNTY OF (2)_____

I, the undersigned, an officer authorized to administer oaths, certify that (3)_____, the testator, and (4)_____, (4)_____, and (4)_____, the witnesses, whose names are signed to the attached or foregoing instrument and whose signatures appear below, having appeared before me and having been first been duly sworn, each then declared to me that: 1) the attached or foregoing instrument is the last Will of the testator; 2) the testator willingly and voluntarily declared, signed, and executed the Will in the presence of the witnesses; 3) the witnesses signed the Will upon the request of the testator, in the presence and hearing of the testator and in the presence of each other; 4) to the best knowledge of each witness, the testator was, at the time of signing, of the age of majority (or otherwise legally competent to make a Will), of sound mind and memory, and under no constrain or undue influence; and, 5) each witness was and is competent and of proper age to witness a Will.

(3)_____[Do Not Sign]_____ (Testator)

(4)_____[Do Not Sign]_____ (Witness)

(4)_____[Do Not Sign]_____ (Witness)

(4)_____[Do Not Sign]_____ (Witness)

Subscribed and sworn to before me by that (3)_____, the testator, who is personally known to me or who has produced a (5)_____ as identification, and by (4)_____, a witness, who is personally known to me or who has produced a (5)_____ as identification, and by (4)_____, a witness, who is personally known to me or who has produced a (5)_____ as identification, and by (4)_____ a witness, who is personally known to me or who has produced a (5)_____ as identification, this this (6)_____ day of _____, 20_____.

(7)_____[Do Not Sign]_____

Notary or other officer

Draft Form C

Self-Proved Will Page—New Hampshire
(attach to Will)

STATE OF NEW HAMPSHIRE

COUNTY OF (2)_____

The foregoing instrument was acknowledged before me this (6)_____ [day], by
(3)_____, the testator; (4)_____,
(4)_____, and (4)_____, the witnesses,
who under oath swear as follows:

1. The testator signed the instrument as his Will or expressly directed another to sign for him.

2. This was the testator's free and voluntary act for the purposes expressed in the Will.

3. Each witness signed at the request of the testator, in his presence, and in the presence of the other witness.

4. To the best of my knowledge, at the time of the signing the testator was at least 18 years of age, or if under 18 years was a married person, and was of sane mind and under no constraint or undue influence.

(5)_____ [Do Not Sign] _____

Signature

_____

Official Capacity

Draft Form D

Self-Proved Will Affidavit—Texas

(attach to Will)

STATE OF TEXAS

COUNTY OF (2)_____

Before me, the undersigned authority, on this day personally appeared (3)_____ (4)_____, (4)_____, and (4)_____, known to me to be the testator and the witnesses, respectively, whose names are subscribed to the annexed or foregoing instrument in their respective capacities, and, all of said persons being by me duly sworn, the said (3)_____ testator, declared to me and to the said witnesses in my presence that said instrument is his or her last Will and testament, and that he or she had willingly made and executed it as his or her free act and deed, and the said witnesses, each on his or her oath stated to me in the presence and hearing of the said testator, that the said testator had declared to them that said instrument is his or her last Will and testament, and that he or she executed same as such and wanted each of them to sign it as a witness; and upon their oaths each witness stated further that they did sign the same as witnesses in the presence of the said testator and at his or her request; that he or she was at the time eighteen years of age or over (or being under such age, was or had been lawfully married, or was then a member of the armed forces of the United States or an auxiliary thereof or of the Maritime Service) and was of sound mind; and that each of said witnesses was then at least fourteen years of age.

(3)_____[Do Not Sign]_____ (Testator)

(4)_____[Do Not Sign]_____ (Witness)

(4)_____[Do Not Sign]_____ (Witness)

(4)_____[Do Not Sign]_____ (Witness)

Subscribed and sworn to before me by (3)_____, the testator, and by (4)_____, (4)_____ and (4)_____ the witnesses, this (6)_____ day of _____, 20_____.

Signed: (5)_____[Do Not Sign]_____

_____
Official Capacity of Officer

Chapter 4:
Your Health Care Advance Directive (Living Will)

Drafting your Will and Financial Power of Attorney (Chapter 5) reflects your sense of responsibility toward your loved ones. Arranging for the treatment you would want in the event of a medical crisis fulfills your responsibility to *yourself*. In this chapter, you will learn the differences between a traditional Living Will and the comprehensive Health Care Advance Directive; how a properly completed directive, with a designated agent, can assure that your wishes are respected; and, how to complete your own directive.

Most people are familiar with the term *Living Will*, even if they are not sure precisely what it means. In fact, legal provisions for carrying out your wishes about health care when you are incapacitated by illness or disease can be found in variously titled documents, such as a "directive to physicians," a "health care declaration," a "medical directive," and others. Since "Living Will" is the most common term, it is used in the title of this book. However, as you will see, the advance directive in this book is more comprehensive than a Living Will, simplifying the process of formalizing your wishes and assuring that they are carried out by someone you trust.

Do not allow the highly charged public debate in this arena to deter you from making your wishes known. You—and only you—must decide the type and extent of treatment you would like to have in a medical emergency, whether it takes the form of an automobile accident when you are 21 years old or terminal cancer when you are a long-lived 91. Likewise, you must decide who will speak for you in such situations, interpreting your instructions for health care providers and facilities.

What is a Health Care Advance Directive?

A traditional *Living Will* is intended to convey the writer's instructions for life-sustaining medical treatment in the event of a terminal illness. If you have a Living Will, you also need a Power of Attorney for Health Care, as you need to name someone to serve as your *agent*. This person, often a spouse, consults the information you have provided to make decisions about your care.

The *Health Care Advance Directive* in this book (prepared by the American Bar Association) integrates the provisions of a Living Will and a Power of Attorney for Health Care into one comprehensive document. The form is clear, easy to complete, and can save you money, time, and possible confusion by addressing your major concerns in a single form. Additionally, it provides an opportunity to make your wishes about organ donation known. It is important to note that, while an advance directive can be invaluable in the declining years of a person's life, it is much more. A directive may become a critical tool for anyone, at any stage of life or state of health. Everyone needs to be prepared for whatever medical emergencies they may encounter in the course of their lives.

Your spiritual, ethical, and moral values will be reflected in the choices you make. In some cases, your concern about the cost to your loved ones—emotional and financial—may affect your decision if you are nearing the end of your life. Regardless of these considerations, worries about the future will be eased if you make your wishes known.

Once you have completed your advance directive, be sure to give copies to your agent, physician, and close family members. Unlike a Will, providing the original is usually unnecessary, as the expressed wishes are what count.

Your Risk without a Directive

Without a Health Care Advance Directive, you risk having decisions made about your medical treatment—such as starting, maintaining, and ending life support systems—that are against your wishes. Although most doctors and health care facilities routinely involve families in making decisions about treatment, problems arise when family members are unaware of what you might wish in a particular situation.

Moreover, your family members may disagree about the right course of action in an emergency. Life-and-death decisions are less traumatic for loved ones to make when they can be guided by your clearly stated wishes. Needless agony can be avoided by observing the legal formalities. Critical and terminal situations are stressful enough for loved ones without the added pressure to make decisions about care without your guidance.

Choosing an Agent

Naming an agent to speak for you when you cannot speak for yourself may be one of the most important decisions you will ever make. You may be, quite literally, putting your life in that person's hands.

Not surprisingly, most people entrust their spouse or an adult child with this responsibility. It is wise to discuss your wishes for treatment and your choice of an agent with your family and any close friends who might be involved. When considering a spouse as a potential agent, one point to consider is whether he or she is likely to be emotionally overwhelmed by your medical crisis. If so, another close relative might be a kinder choice. Of course, this assumes that all family members are comfortable with your wishes and would agree on interpreting them.

As with the executor of your Will and your agent in financial matters, trusting that your wishes will be carried out is paramount in choosing an agent. Normally, no one else will oversee or monitor you agent's decisions.

In your directive, you can define the degree of authority you would like for your agent to have. Generally, broad is better than limited, as it is more likely to give your decision-maker the authority to carry out your wishes in unforeseen situations. In addition, you can name alternative agents (two is safest) in the event that your first choice is not available. You can also disqualify specific individuals whom you would not want to serve, if that is a worrisome issue.

Your agent will serve as your spokesperson, analyzer, legal decision-maker, interpreter, and advocate. Make your choice after careful consideration. If there is not anyone that you would feel comfortable naming at this time, it is safer to not name anyone at all. The information you provide will be used to guide your treatment. In the absence of an official representative, physicians and health care institutions have a legal obligation to abide by your stated wishes.

If You Change Your Mind

You can change or cancel your directive at any time. It is best to immediately notify anyone who has a copy of the old directive, especially your agent and physician. Destroy all copies of the old directive and make a new one without delay. Remember, everyone needs to have their wishes known, as well as someone legally designated to carry those wishes out.

Keeping Loved Ones Informed

Your carefully considered planning will all be for naught if your agent, physician, and health care center do not have copies of your directive to guide their decisions regarding your treatment. In this case, a copy is fine, but it should be readily available. The contents should not come as a surprise to loved ones.

Organ Donation

An increasing number of people are considering *organ donation* as an opportunity to make a unique charitable contribution. Their relatives often find solace in the fact that other lives will be saved as a result of this generous decision. In this way, particularly, meaning may be brought to senseless tragedies, such as the sudden loss of loved ones in the prime of life.

The directive in this book offers several options for those who are interested in making anatomical gifts when they die. While major organs for transplant may come immediately to mind, there is potential for saving and improving many more lives with a broader directive. Skin tissue, for example, is used in the treatment of burn victims, corneas are used to restore eyesight, and much more.

Like all the major decisions discussed, organ donation is a highly personal choice that no one should have to make for you. The form in this book makes it easy to specify your wishes, taking any restrictions into consideration.

An Example of the
Living Will Health Care Advance Directive

Now look at the sample, filled-in form on page 92 to see how the Health Care Advance Directive works. It is based on the following situation.

John Smith has been married to Mary Smith for forty years. They have two adult children, David Smith, a stockbroker, and Ann Smith, a nurse. John does not want his life prolonged by medical treatment if the treatment will not give him the ability to think and communicate with others. He has discussed, many times, his wishes with Mary, David, and Ann. John trusts his family to follow his wishes. He is comfortable appointing his wife, Mary, then nurse daughter, Ann, then stockbroker son, David, to be his health care agent without any specific instructions. John also wants his organs donated for medical purposes.

Publisher's Note: *The following form is reprinted by permission of the American Bar Association. While sample, filled-in information has been added for instructional purposes, the form has not otherwise been altered. Any formatting, layout, or typographical errors or inconsistencies are as contained in the original form.*

Health Care Advance Directive
Part I *Appointment of Health Care Agent*

1.   HEALTH CARE AGENT

I, _____ John Smith _____ hereby appoint:
        PRINCIPAL

_____ Mary Smith _____
        AGENT'S NAME

_____ 1 Any Street, Any City, Any State _____
        ADDRESS

_____ 555-555-1234 _____   _____ 555-555-1235 _____
HOME PHONE#   WORK PHONE#

as my agent to make health and personal care decisions for me as authorized in this document.

2.   ALTERNATE AGENTS

IF
- I revoke my Agent's authority; or
- my Agent becomes unwilling or unavailable to act; or
- if my agent is my spouse and I become legally separated or divorced,

I name the following (each to act alone and successively, in the order named) as alternates to my Agent:

A. First Alternate Agent _____ Ann Jones _____

   Address 2 Any Street, Any City, Any State _____

   Telephone 555-555-1236 _____

B. Second Alternate Agent_____ David Smith _____

   Address 3 Any Street, Any City, Any State _____

   Telephone 555-555-1237 _____

3. EFFECTIVE DATE AND DURABILITY

By this document I intend to create a health care advance directive. It is effective upon, and only during, any period in which I cannot make or communicate a choice regarding a particular health care decision. My agent, attending physician and any other necessary experts should determine that I am unable to make choices about health care.

4. AGENT'S POWERS

I give my Agent full authority to make health care decisions for me. My Agent shall follow my wishes as known to my Agent either through this document or through other means. When my agent interprets my wishes, I intend my Agent's authority to be as broad as possible, except for any limitations I state in this form. In making any decision, my Agent shall try to discuss the proposed decision with me to determine my desires if I am able to communicate in any way. If my Agent cannot determine the choice I would want, then my Agent shall make a choice for me based upon what my Agent believes to be in my best interests.

Unless specifically limited by Section 6, below, my Agent is authorized as follows:

A. To consent, refuse, or withdraw consent to any and all types of health care. Health care means any care, treatment, service or procedure to maintain, diagnose or otherwise affect an individual's physical or mental condition. It includes, but is not limited to, artificial respiration, nutritional support and hydration, medication and cardiopulmonary resuscitation;

B. To have access to medical records and information to the same extent that I am entitled, including the right to disclose the contents to others as appropriate for my health care;

C. To authorize my admission to or discharge (even against medical advice) from any hospital, nursing home, residential care, assisted living or similar facility or service;

D. To contract on my behalf for any health care related service or facility on my behalf, without my Agent incurring personal financial liability for such contracts;

E. To hire and fire medical, social service, and other support personnel responsible for my care;

F. To authorize, or refuse to authorize, any medication or procedure intended to relieve pain, even though such use may lead to physical damage, addiction, or hasten the moment of (but not intentionally cause) my death;

G. To make anatomical gifts of part or all of my body for medical purposes, authorize an autopsy, and direct the disposition of my remains, to the extent permitted by law;

H. To take any other action necessary to do what I authorize here, including (but not limited to) granting any waiver or release from liability required by any hospital, physician, or other health care provider; signing any documents relating to refusals of treatment or the leaving of a facility against medical advice; and pursuing any legal action in my name at the expense of my estate to force compliance with my wishes as determined by my Agent, or to seek actual or punitive damages for the failure to comply.

Health Care Advance Directive
Part II   *Instructions About Health Care*

5.   MY INSTRUCTIONS ABOUT END-OF-LIFE TREATMENT

(Initial only ONE of the following statements)

__JS__   **NO SPECIFIC INSTRUCTIONS.** My agent knows my values and wishes, so I do not wish to include any specific instructions here.

_____   **DIRECTIVE TO WITHHOLD OR WITHDRAW TREATMENT.** Although I greatly value life, I also believe that at some point, life has such diminished value that medical treatment should be stopped, and I should be allowed to die. Therefore, I do not want to receive treatment, including nutrition and hydration, when the treatment will not give me a meaningful quality of life. I do not want my life prolonged...

_____   ... if the treatment will leave me in a condition of permanent unconsciousness, such as with an irreversible coma or a persistent vegetative state.

_____   ... if the treatment will leave me with no more than some consciousness and in an irreversible condition of complete, or nearly complete, loss of ability to think or communicate with others.

_____   ... if the treatment will leave me with no more than some ability to think or communicate with others, and the likely risks and burdens of treatment outweigh the expected benefits. Risks, burdens and benefits include consideration of length of life, quality of life, financial costs, and my personal dignity and privacy.

_____   **DIRECTIVE TO RECEIVE TREATMENT.** I want my life to be prolonged as long as possible, no matter what my quality of life.

_____   **DIRECTIVE ABOUT END-OF-LIFE TREATMENT IN MY OWN WORDS:**

_____

_____

_____

_____

_____

6. ANY OTHER HEALTH CARE INSTRUCTIONS OR LIMITATIONS OR MODIFICATIONS OF MY AGENTS POWERS

_____

_____

_____

_____

7. PROTECTION OF THIRD PARTIES WHO RELY ON MY AGENT

No person who relies in good faith upon any representations by my Agent or Alternate Agent(s) shall be liable to me, my estate, my heirs or assigns, for recognizing the Agent's authority.

8. DONATION OF ORGANS AT DEATH

Upon my death:
(Initial one)

_____ I do *not* wish to donate any organs or tissue, OR

__JS__ I give *any* needed organs, tissues, or parts, OR

_____ I give *only* the following organs, tissues, or parts:
(please specify)

_____

_____

My gift (if any) is for the following purposes:
(Cross out any of the following you do not want)

■ Transplant
■ Research
■ Therapy
■ Education

9.   NOMINATION OF GUARDIAN

If a guardian of my person should for any reason need to be appointed, I nominate my Agent (or his or her alternate then authorized to act), named above.

10.   ADMINISTRATIVE PROVISIONS

(All apply)

- I revoke any prior health care advance directive.
- This health care advance directive is intended to be valid in any jurisdiction in which it is presented.
- A copy of this advance directive is intended to have the same effect as the original.

SIGNING THE DOCUMENT

BY SIGNING HERE I INDICATE THAT I UNDERSTAND THE CONTENTS OF THIS DOCUMENT AND THE EFFECT OF THIS GRANT OF POWERS TO MY AGENT.

I sign my name to this Health Care Advance Directive on this

__1st__ day of _____December_____ , 20 _06_ .

My Signature _*John Smith*_____

My Name__John Smith_____

My current home address is__1 Any Street, Any City, Any State_____

_____

_____

_____

WITNESS STATEMENT

I declare that the person who signed or acknowledged this document is personally known to me, that he/she signed or acknowledged this health care advance directive in my presence, and that he/she appears to be of sound mind and under no duress, fraud, or undue influence.

I am not:

- the person appointed as agent by this document,
- the principal's health care provider,
- an employee of the principal's health care provider,
- financially responsible for the principal's health care,
- related to the principal by blood, marriage, or adoption, and,
- to the best of my knowledge, a creditor of the principal/or entitled to any part of his/her estate under a will now existing or by operation of law.

Witness #1:

First Witness _____ December 1, 2006
Signature _____ Date

First Witness _____
Print Name

555-555-1238 _____
Telephone

4 Any Street, Any City, Any State _____
Residence Address

Witness #2:

Second Witness _____ December 1, 2006
Signature _____ Date

Second Witness _____
Print Name

555-555-1239 _____
Telephone

5 Any Street, Any City, Any State _____
Residence Address

NOTARIZATION

STATE OF _____ Any State _____)

COUNTY OF _____ Any County _____)

On this 1st day of ___ December ___, 20 06,

the said _____ John Smith _____, known to me (or satisfactorily proven) to be the person named in the foregoing instrument, personally appeared before me, a Notary Public, within and for the State and County aforesaid, and acknowledged that he or she freely and voluntarily executed the same for the purposes stated therein.

My Commission Expires: 12/30/06

Any Notary _____
NOTARY PUBLIC

A Conversation about Health Care Advance Directives

Client:

I trust my family to make the right decisions about my care. Is having a formal directive really necessary?

Lawyer:

Your wishes are more likely to be followed if you have an advance directive, even if you're surrounded by loving relatives. Are you certain you've communicated your wishes clearly? Can you guarantee that all your loved ones would agree about what you would want done in a particular situation? Without a directive, not only do you risk not having your wishes honored, but you may unwittingly set the stage for rifts within your family.

Client:

My brother has a Living Will. Is that enough to serve his purposes?

Lawyer:

No. Living Wills are helpful because they state your wishes. The problem is that your brother also needs an agent—a Power of Attorney for Health Care—to carry out those wishes. Also, Living Will forms have traditionally focused on care during the final stage of life. Actually, most decisions on medical treatment involve patients of all ages who may be critical, but not terminal. Every adult should have an advance directive.

Client:

In our family discussion, my cousin, who believes in prolonging life under any circumstances, said she was grateful she had good health insurance!

Lawyer:

She may not have thought through that aspect of prolonging life when there is virtually no hope of improvement, let alone recovery. Insurance companies put a cap on the maximum they will pay for an illness, and in hospitals today, that cap can be reached fairly quickly when the patient is on life support systems. Your cousin might not want her family to go bankrupt to pay for her care.

Client:

What do you recommend as the best way to go about making these potentially life-and-death decisions and drawing up an Advance Directive for Health Care?

Lawyer:

You've started by discussing the subject within your family. Continue serious conversations with your spouse and other loved ones. You may want to talk with your physician to make sure you understand exactly what your choices would mean. After careful consideration, follow the instructions for filling out the directive, and give copies to your agent (usually your spouse), other closely involved family members, and your physician.

Instructions for Completing the Draft Health Care Advance Directive Form

Since the Health Care Advance Directive directs the user to what information to include and where to fill it in on the form, the instructions for completing it are slightly different from those of other forms in the book.

Section 1—Health Care Agent

(1) Print your full name here as the *principal* (or creator) of the Health Care Advance Directive.

(2) Print the full name, address, and telephone number of the person (age 18 or older) you appoint as your health care agent. Appoint *only* a person with whom you have talked and whom you trust to understand and carry out your values and wishes.

Many states limit the persons who can serve as your agent. If you want to meet all existing state restrictions *do not* name any of the following as your agent, since some states will not let them act in that role:

- your health care providers, including physicians;
- staff of health care facilities or nursing care facilities providing your care;
- guardians of your finances (also called conservators);
- employees of government agencies financially responsible for your care; or,
- any person serving as agent for ten or more persons.

Section 2—Alternate Agents

(3) It is a good idea to name alternate agents in case your first agent is not available. Of course, only appoint alternates if you fully trust them to act faithfully as your agent and you have talked to them about serving as your agent. Print the appropriate information in this paragraph. You can name as many alternate agents as you wish, but place them in the order you wish them to serve.

Section 3—Effective Date and Durability

This sample document is effective if and when you cannot make health care decisions. Your agent and your doctor determine if you are in this condition. Some state laws include specific procedures for determining your decision-making ability. If you wish, you can include other effective dates or other criteria for determining that you cannot make health care decisions (such as requiring two physicians to evaluate your decision-making ability). You can also state that the power will end at some later date or event before death.

In any case, you have the *right to revoke*—or take away—the agent's authority at any time. To revoke, notify your agent or health care provider orally or in writing. If you revoke, it is best to notify in writing both your agent and physician and anyone else who has a copy of the directive. Also, destroy the Health Care Advance Directive document itself.

Section 4—Agent's Powers

This grant of power is intended to be as broad as possible. Unless you set limits, your agent will have authority to make any decision you could make to obtain or stop any type of health care.

Even under this broad grant of authority, your agent still must follow your wishes and directions, communicated by you in any manner now or in the future. To specifically limit or direct your agent's power, you must complete Section 6 in Part II of the advance directive.

Section 5—My Instructions About End-of-Life Treatment

(4) The subject of end-of-life treatment is particularly important to many people. In this paragraph, you can give general or specific instructions on the subject. The different paragraphs are options—*choose only one*—or write your desires or instructions in your own words (in the last option). If you are satisfied with your agent's knowledge of your values and wishes and you do not want to include instructions in the form, initial the first option and do not give instructions in the form.

Any instructions you give here will guide your agent. If you do not appoint an agent, they will guide any health care providers or surrogate decision-makers who must make a decision for you if you cannot do so yourself. The instruction choices in the form describe different treatment goals you may prefer, depending on your condition.

Section 6—Any Other Health Care Instructions, Limitations, or Modifications of My Agent's Powers

(5) In this section, you can provide instructions about other health care issues that are not end-of-life treatment or nutrition and hydration. For example, you might want to include your wishes about non-emergency surgery, elective

medical treatments, or admission to a nursing home. Again, be careful in these instructions not to place limitations on your agent that you do not intend. For example, while you may not want to be admitted to a nursing home, placing such a restriction may make things impossible for your agent if other options are not available.

You also may limit your agent's powers in any way you wish. For example, you can instruct your agent to refuse any specific types of treatment that are against your religious beliefs or are unacceptable to you for any other reasons. These might include blood transfusions, electroconvulsive therapy, sterilization, abortion, amputation, psychosurgery, or admission to a mental institution. Some states limit your agent's authority to consent to or refuse some of these procedures, regardless of your Health Care Advance Directive.

Be very careful about stating limitations, because the specific circumstances surrounding future health care decisions are impossible to predict. If you do not want any limitations, simply write in "No limitations."

Section 7—Protection of Third Parties Who Rely on My Agent

In most states, health care providers cannot be forced to follow the directions of your agent if they object. However, most states also require providers to help transfer you to another provider who is willing to honor your instructions. To encourage compliance with the Health Care Advance Directive, this paragraph states that providers who rely in good faith on the agent's statements and decisions will not be held civilly liable for their actions.

Section 8—Donation of Organs at Death

(6) In this section you can state your intention to donate bodily organs and tissues at death. If you do not wish to be an organ donor, initial the first option. The second option is a donation of any or all organs or parts. The third option allows you to donate only those organs or tissues you specify. Consider mentioning the heart, liver, lung, kidney, pancreas, intestine, cornea, bone, skin, heart valves, tendons, ligaments, and saphenous vein in the leg. Finally, you may limit the use of your organs by *crossing out* any of the four purposes listed that you do not want your organs used for (transplant, therapy, research, or education). If you do not cross out any of these options, your organs may be used for any of these purposes.

Section 9—Nomination of Guardian

Appointing a health care agent helps to avoid a court-appointed guardian for health care decision-making. However, if a court becomes involved for any reason, this paragraph expressly names your agent to serve as guardian. A court does not have to follow your nomination, but normally it will honor your wishes unless there is good reason to override your choice.

Section 10—Administrative Provisions

These items address miscellaneous matters that could affect the implementation of your Health Care Advance Directive.

Signing the Document

(7) and (9) You must sign and date the document for it to be effective. It should be signed in front of a notary public to help alleviate any future problems.

(8) Your witnesses should know your identity personally and be able to declare that you appear to be of sound mind and under no duress or undue influence.

In order to meet the different witnessing requirements of most states, *do not* have the following people witness your signature.

- Anyone you have chosen to make health care decisions on your behalf (agent or alternate agents).
- Your treating physician, health care provider, health facility operator, or an employee of any of these.
- Insurers or employees of your life/health insurance provider.
- Anyone financially responsible for your health care costs.
- Anyone related to you by blood, marriage, or adoption.
- Anyone entitled to any part of your estate under an existing Will or by operation of law, or anyone who will benefit financially from your death. Your creditors should not serve as witnesses.

Caution: This Health Care Advance Directive is a general form provided for your convenience. While it meets the legal requirements of most states, it may or may not fit the requirements of your particular state. Many states have special forms or special procedures for creating Health Care Advance Directives. Even if your state's law does not clearly recognize this document, it may still provide an effective statement of your wishes if you cannot speak for yourself.

Health Care Advance Directive
Part I *Appointment of Health Care Agent*

1.   HEALTH CARE AGENT

I, _____ hereby appoint:
        PRINCIPAL

_____
        AGENT'S NAME

_____
        ADDRESS

_____
  HOME PHONE#   WORK PHONE#

as my agent to make health and personal care decisions for me as authorized in this document.

2.   ALTERNATE AGENTS

IF
- I revoke my Agent's authority; or
- my Agent becomes unwilling or unavailable to act; or
- if my agent is my spouse and I become legally separated or divorced,

I name the following (each to act alone and successively, in the order named) as alternates to my Agent:

A. First Alternate Agent _____

    Address_____

    Telephone_____

B. Second Alternate Agent _____

    Address _____

    Telephone _____

3. EFFECTIVE DATE AND DURABILITY

By this document I intend to create a health care advance directive. It is effective upon, and only during, any period in which I cannot make or communicate a choice regarding a particular health care decision. My agent, attending physician and any other necessary experts should determine that I am unable to make choices about health care.

4. AGENT'S POWERS

I give my Agent full authority to make health care decisions for me. My Agent shall follow my wishes as known to my Agent either through this document or through other means. When my agent interprets my wishes, I intend my Agent's authority to be as broad as possible, except for any limitations I state in this form. In making any decision, my Agent shall try to discuss the proposed decision with me to determine my desires if I am able to communicate in any way. If my Agent cannot determine the choice I would want, then my Agent shall make a choice for me based upon what my Agent believes to be in my best interests.

Unless specifically limited by Section 6, below, my Agent is authorized as follows:

A. To consent, refuse, or withdraw consent to any and all types of health care. Health care means any care, treatment, service or procedure to maintain, diagnose or otherwise affect an individual's physical or mental condition. It includes, but is not limited to, artificial respiration, nutritional support and hydration, medication and cardiopulmonary resuscitation;

B. To have access to medical records and information to the same extent that I am entitled, including the right to disclose the contents to others as appropriate for my health care;

C. To authorize my admission to or discharge (even against medical advice) from any hospital, nursing home, residential care, assisted living or similar facility or service;

D. To contract on my behalf for any health care related service or facility on my behalf, without my Agent incurring personal financial liability for such contracts;

E. To hire and fire medical, social service, and other support personnel responsible for my care;

F. To authorize, or refuse to authorize, any medication or procedure intended to relieve pain, even though such use may lead to physical damage, addiction, or hasten the moment of (but not intentionally cause) my death;

G. To make anatomical gifts of part or all of my body for medical purposes, authorize an autopsy, and direct the disposition of my remains, to the extent permitted by law;

H. To take any other action necessary to do what I authorize here, including (but not limited to) granting any waiver or release from liability required by any hospital, physician, or other health care provider; signing any documents relating to refusals of treatment or the leaving of a facility against medical advice; and pursuing any legal action in my name at the expense of my estate to force compliance with my wishes as determined by my Agent, or to seek actual or punitive damages for the failure to comply.

Health Care Advance Directive
Part II   *Instructions About Health Care*

5.   MY INSTRUCTIONS ABOUT END-OF-LIFE TREATMENT

(Initial only ONE of the following statements)

_____   **NO SPECIFIC INSTRUCTIONS.** My agent knows my values and wishes, so I do not wish to include any specific instructions here.

DIRECTIVE TO WITHHOLD OR WITHDRAW TREATMENT. Although I greatly value life, I also believe that at some point, life has such diminished value that medical treatment should be stopped, and I should be allowed to die. Therefore, I do not want to receive treatment, including nutrition and hydration, when the treatment will not give me a meaningful quality of life. I do not want my life prolonged...

_____   ... if the treatment will leave me in a condition of permanent unconsciousness, such as with an irreversible coma or a persistent vegetative state.

_____   ... if the treatment will leave me with no more than some consciousness and in an irreversible condition of complete, or nearly complete, loss of ability to think or communicate with others.

_____   ... if the treatment will leave me with no more than some ability to think or communicate with others, and the likely risks and burdens of treatment outweigh the expected benefits. Risks, burdens and benefits include consideration of length of life, quality of life, financial costs, and my personal dignity and privacy.

_____   **DIRECTIVE TO RECEIVE TREATMENT.** I want my life to be prolonged as long as possible, no matter what my quality of life.

_____   **DIRECTIVE ABOUT END-OF-LIFE TREATMENT IN MY OWN WORDS:**

_____

_____

_____

_____

_____

6. ANY OTHER HEALTH CARE INSTRUCTIONS OR LIMITATIONS OR MODIFICATIONS OF MY AGENTS POWERS

_____

_____

_____

_____

7. PROTECTION OF THIRD PARTIES WHO RELY ON MY AGENT

No person who relies in good faith upon any representations by my Agent or Alternate Agent(s) shall be liable to me, my estate, my heirs or assigns, for recognizing the Agent's authority.

8. DONATION OF ORGANS AT DEATH

Upon my death:
(Initial one)

_____ I do *not* wish to donate any organs or tissue, OR

_____ I give *any* needed organs, tissues, or parts, OR

_____ I give *only* the following organs, tissues, or parts:
(please specify)

_____

_____

My gift (if any) is for the following purposes:
(Cross out any of the following you do not want)

■ Transplant
■ Research
■ Therapy
■ Education

9.   NOMINATION OF GUARDIAN

If a guardian of my person should for any reason need to be appointed, I nominate my Agent (or his or her alternate then authorized to act), named above.

10.   ADMINISTRATIVE PROVISIONS

   (All apply)

- I revoke any prior health care advance directive.
- This health care advance directive is intended to be valid in any jurisdiction in which it is presented.
- A copy of this advance directive is intended to have the same effect as the original.

SIGNING THE DOCUMENT

BY SIGNING HERE I INDICATE THAT I UNDERSTAND THE CONTENTS OF THIS DOCUMENT AND THE EFFECT OF THIS GRANT OF POWERS TO MY AGENT.

I sign my name to this Health Care Advance Directive on this

_____ day of _____, 20_____.

My Signature_____

My Name_____

My current home address is_____

_____

_____

_____

WITNESS STATEMENT

I declare that the person who signed or acknowledged this document is personally known to me, that he/she signed or acknowledged this health care advance directive in my presence, and that he/she appears to be of sound mind and under no duress, fraud, or undue influence.

I am not:
- the person appointed as agent by this document,
- the principal's health care provider,
- an employee of the principal's health care provider,
- financially responsible for the principal's health care,
- related to the principal by blood, marriage, or adoption, and,
- to the best of my knowledge, a creditor of the principal/or entitled to any part of his/her estate under a will now existing or by operation of law.

Witness #1:

_____
Signature   Date

_____
Print Name

_____
Telephone

_____
Residence Address

Witness #2:

_____
Signature   Date

_____
Print Name

_____
Telephone

_____
Residence Address

NOTARIZATION

STATE OF _____)

COUNTY OF _____)

On this ____ day of _____, 20___,

the said _____,
known to me (or satisfactorily proven) to be the person named in the foregoing instrument, personally appeared before me, a Notary Public, within and for the State and County aforesaid, and acknowledged that he or she freely and voluntarily executed the same for the purposes stated therein.

My Commission Expires:

_____
NOTARY PUBLIC

Chapter 5:
Your Power of Attorney for Finances

Now that you have prepared your Will and Living Will, the next step in planning for your future is preparing a Power of Attorney for Finances. The order of your business and personal life can quickly turn to chaos without someone to make day-to-day decisions and act in your stead—from paying bills to filing taxes. In this chapter, you learn the duties of an agent under a Power of Attorney; how to complete the appropriate form and safeguard its use; and, how to ensure that it will be honored by your bank and other financial institutions.

What is a Power of Attorney?

A *Power of Attorney* is a legal document that authorizes your representative, or *agent*, to act on your behalf in financial matters. As the purpose of this book is to provide you with the legal tools to protect your interests when you cannot act on your own, this chapter focuses on a *General Power of Attorney*, which allows your agent to manage all of your financial affairs during your lifetime.

Neither businesses nor households run smoothly if bills are not paid on time. Other typical financial tasks that agents perform include buying, selling, or managing real estate; monitoring investments and retirement plans; overseeing the management of a business; and, handling accounting and tax matters. While some tasks are fairly routine, others may be quite complex, requiring sound business sense. For this type of agent, good intentions and willingness to serve may not be enough to assure your family's financial health—so choose one with great care.

The authority you grant your agent should be broad, in order not to hinder the efficient performance of all anticipated duties. Since the Power of Attorney form you sign today is meant to be enacted in the future, plan for any possible contingencies you can. However, if you wish, you can specify financial areas in which your agent may not act.

Your Risk without a Power of Attorney

Without a Power of Attorney, your family might have to go to court to have a guardian appointed to take care of your financial affairs. Without a qualified person designated in advance in a Power of Attorney, not even the most routine transactions can take place.

As with most court proceedings, this will take time and there will be the expense of a lawyer's fee. Additionally, the court may not select the person you would have named to manage your finances. If, on the other hand, you have already given your agent a Power of Attorney, the court will not be involved in your financial affairs; they will not be disrupted; and, someone in whom you have absolute faith will be in a position to protect your interests.

Choosing Your Agent

Choosing an agent to exercise authority over your bank and investment accounts for an indefinite period is of the utmost importance. Many people name their spouse or another family member—someone they completely trust.

There is, however, another critical consideration. Does the person you have in mind have the ability to handle finances? You may trust your choice not to clean out your bank accounts, but if he or she never manages to balance the family checkbook, you may want to give the matter more thought. Unfortunately, an agent does not have to be dishonest to send you into financial ruin—just incompetent.

Remember, you will be legally bound by what your agent does through the Power of Attorney. However, while some have called it a *license to steal*, your agent is not free to do anything he or she chooses. Your agent will have a *fiduciary* relationship with you, and is therefore legally required to act only in your best interests. Still, you need to exercise caution in making your choice, even when dealing with family members.

As soon as your Financial Power of Attorney is signed, it is legally valid. While this is an advantage in that financial matters can be attended to without delay, it means there is yet another reason for having complete faith in your agent. You might consider keeping the original Power of Attorney (which is required to be presented), in your possession in a safe place. Your agent should know this location, and it should be fairly accessible when needed.

Honoring a Financial Power of Attorney

A critical point to consider when you prepare your Financial Power of Attorney is whether your bank and other financial institutions will honor it. Historically, this has been an important issue, as many institutions have their own forms and sometimes refuse to honor a Power of Attorney on a form that is not their own. Considering the power conveyed in this document, this attitude is understandable.

There has recently been progress in developing a Power of Attorney form that could be used in every state, aimed at simplifying the process and increasing the likelihood of acceptance by financial institutions. The form in this book is state-of-the-art in this regard, having been derived from a uniform model law drafted by the National Conference of Commissioners on Uniform State Laws.

Completing the Form

Once you know who your agent is, the form is easy to fill out. It contains instructions in it. Most people *do not* withhold individual powers from their agent. Initial the blank labeled "N," as done in the sample, and you are finished except for signing and notarizing your filled-in document.

However, you may not want your agent, for example, to be able to sell your home or trade in commodities. In that case, the form allows you to initial the powers you are granting and to withhold powers by either not initialing the power or crossing out the power you want to withhold.

The block for "Special Instructions" can be used to tell your agent of specific tasks you wish him or her to perform. For example, you may wish an agent to pay your mother's bills or pay to stable your horse.

The following two forms are:
1. a sample, filled-in complete Power of Attorney form, which contains the listing of powers given, along with legal definitions of the powers (this listing is tedious, but it is best to read) and
2. blank form without the legal definitions, on which you can prepare your draft. The final form you need to fill out and take to a notary, appears in the Appendix.

An Example of the Power of Attorney

Examine the sample, filled-in form on page 115 to see how the Power of Attorney works. It is based on the following situation.

John Smith has been married to Mary Smith for forty years. They have two adult children. John owns most of his financial assets (his home, bank accounts, stock brokerage accounts) jointly with Mary. He owns a small stock brokerage account, inherited from his father, in his own name. John wants Mary to have complete control over this account, as well as any other financial assets he may own in the future.

SAMPLE, FILLED-IN FORM

Power of Attorney

I _____John Smith_____ of _____Any City_____, _____Any State_____
appoint _____Mary Smith_____ of _____Any City_____, _____Any State_____
as my agent to act for me in any lawful way with respect to the following initialed subjects:

TO GRANT ALL OF THE FOLLOWING POWERS, INITIAL THE LINE IN FRONT OF (N) AND IGNORE THE LINES IN FRONT OF THE OTHER POWERS.

TO GRANT ONE OR MORE, BUT FEWER THAN ALL, OF THE FOLLOWING POWERS, INITIAL THE LINE IN FRONT OF EACH POWER YOU ARE GRANTING.

TO WITHHOLD A POWER, DO NOT INITIAL THE LINE IN FRONT OF IT. YOU MAY, BUT NEED NOT, CROSS OUT EACH POWER WITHHELD.

INITIAL

_____ (A)   Real property transactions.

_____ (B)   Tangible personal property transactions.

_____ (C)   Stock and bond transactions.

_____ (D)   Commodity and option transactions.

_____ (E)   Banking and other financial institution transactions.

_____ (F)   Business operating transactions.

_____ (G)   Insurance and annuity transactions.

_____ (H)   Estate, trust, and other beneficiary transactions.

_____ (I)   Claims and litigation.

_____ (J)   Personal and family maintenance.

_____ (K)   Benefits from Social Security, Medicare, Medicaid, or other governmental programs, or military service.

_____ (L)   Retirement plan transactions.

_____ (M)   Tax matters.

__JS__ (N)   ALL OF THE POWERS LISTED ABOVE. YOU NEED NOT INITIAL ANY OTHER LINES IF YOU INITIAL LINE (N).

ON THE FOLLOWING LINES YOU MAY GIVE SPECIAL INSTRUCTIONS LIMITING OR EXTENDING THE POWERS GRANTED TO YOUR AGENT.

_____ No Specific Instructions Given _____

_____

_____

UNLESS YOU DIRECT OTHERWISE ABOVE, THIS POWER OF ATTORNEY IS EFFECTIVE IMMEDIATELY AND WILL CONTINUE UNTIL IT IS REVOKED

This power of attorney will continue to be effective even though I become disabled, incapacitated, or incompetent.

I agree that any third party who receives a copy of this document may act under it. Revocation of the power of attorney is not effective as to a third party until the third party learns of the revocation. I agree to indemnify the third party for any claims that arise against the third party because of reliance on this power of attorney.

Signed this __1st__ day of ____December____, 20 _06_ .

_____*John Smith*_____
[John Smith's Signature]

_____000-00-0000_____
[John Smith's Social Security Number]

WITNESSES:

_____*First Witness*_____
[Signature of Witness]

_____First Witness_____
[Name]

_____4 Any Street_____
[Address]

_____Any City, Any State_____
[Address]

_____*Second Witness*_____
[Signature of Witness]

_____Second Witness_____
[Name]

_____5 Any Street_____
[Address]

_____Any City, Any State_____
[Address]

State of _____Any State_____)

County of _____Any County_____)

This document was acknowledged before me on _____December 1, 2006_____ by

_____John Smith_____ ,   _____First Witness_____ ,   _____Second Witness_____ ,

[Name of Principal]   [Name of Witness]   [Name of Witness]

_____*Any Notary*_____

[Signature of Notarial Officer]

[Seal, if any]

_____Notary Public_____

[Title (and Rank)]

My commission expires: _____12/30/08_____

BY ACCEPTING OR ACTING UNDER THE APPOINTMENT, THE AGENT ASSUMES THE FIDUCIARY AND OTHER LEGAL RESPONSIBILITIES OF AN AGENT.

CONSTRUCTION OF POWERS GENERALLY. By executing a statutory power of attorney, the principal, except as limited or extended by the principal in the power of attorney, empowers the agent, for that subject to:

(1) demand, receive, and obtain by litigation or otherwise, money or other thing of value to which the principal is, may become, or claims to be entitled; and conserve, invest, disburse, or use anything so received for the purposes intended;

(2) contract in any manner with any person, on terms agreeable to the agent, to accomplish a purpose of a transaction, and perform, rescind, reform, release, or modify the contract or another contract made by or on behalf of the principal;

(3) execute, acknowledge, seal, and deliver a deed, revocation, mortgage, lease, notice, check, release, or other instrument the agent considers desirable to accomplish a purpose of a transaction;

(4) prosecute, defend, submit to arbitration, settle, and propose or accept a compromise with respect to, a claim existing in favor of or against the principal or intervene in litigation relating to the claim;

(5) seek on the principal's behalf the assistance of a court to carry out an act authorized by the power of attorney;

(6) engage, compensate, and discharge an attorney, accountant, expert witness, or other assistant;

(7) keep appropriate records of each transaction, including an accounting of receipts and disbursements;

(8) prepare, execute, and file a record, report, or other document the agent considers desirable to safeguard or promote the principal's interest under a statute or governmental regulation;

(9) reimburse the agent for expenditures properly made by the agent in exercising the powers granted by the power of attorney; and

(10) in general, do any other lawful act with respect to the subject.

DEFINITIONS OF POWERS:

A. Real property transactions. The language granting power with respect to real property transactions empowers the agent to:

(1) accept as a gift or as security for a loan, reject, demand, buy, lease, receive, or otherwise acquire, an interest in real property or a right incident to real property;

(2) sell, exchange, convey with or without covenants, quitclaim, release, surrender, mortgage, encumber, partition, consent to partitioning, subdivide, apply for zoning, rezoning, or other governmental permits, plat or consent to platting, develop, grant options concerning, lease, sublease, or otherwise dispose of, an interest in real property or a right incident to real property;

(3) release, assign, satisfy, and enforce by litigation or otherwise, a mortgage, deed of trust, encumbrance, lien, or other claim to real property which exists or is asserted;

(4) do any act of management or of conservation with respect to an interest in real property, or a right incident to real property, owned, or claimed to be owned, by the principal, including:

    (i) insuring against a casualty, liability, or loss;

    (ii) obtaining or regaining possession, or protecting the interest or right, by litigation or otherwise;

    (iii) paying, compromising, or contesting taxes or assessments, or applying for and receiving refunds in connection with them; and

    (iv) purchasing supplies, hiring assistance or labor, and making repairs or alterations in the real property;

(5) use, develop, alter, replace, remove, erect, or install structures or other improvements upon real property in or incident to which the principal has, or claims to have, an interest or right;

(6) participate in a reorganization with respect to real property or a legal entity that owns an interest in or right incident to real property and receive and hold shares of stock or obligations received in a plan of reorganization, and act with respect to them, including:

    (i) selling or otherwise disposing of them;

    (ii) exercising or selling an option, conversion, or similar right with respect to them; and

    (iii) voting them in person or by proxy;

(7) change the form of title of an interest in or right incident to real property;

(8) dedicate to public use, with or without consideration, easements or other real property in which the principal has, or claims to have, an interest.

B. Tangible personal property transactions. The language granting power with respect to tangible personal property transactions empowers the agent to:

(1) accept as a gift or as security for a loan, reject, demand, buy, receive, or otherwise acquire ownership or possession of tangible personal property or an interest in tangible personal property;

(2) sell, exchange, convey with or without covenants, release, surrender, mortgage, encumber, pledge, hypothecate, create a security interest in, pawn, grant options concerning, lease, sublease to others, or otherwise dispose of tangible personal property or an interest in tangible personal property;

(3) release, assign, satisfy, or enforce by litigation or otherwise, a mortgage, security interest, encumbrance, lien, or other claim on behalf of the principal, with respect to tangible personal property or an interest in tangible personal property; and

(4) do an act of management or conservation with respect to tangible personal property or an interest in tangible personal property on behalf of the principal, including:

    (i) insuring against casualty, liability, or loss;

    (ii) obtaining or regaining possession, or protecting the property or interest, by litigation or otherwise;

    (iii) paying, compromising, or contesting taxes or assessments or applying for and receiving refunds in connection with taxes or assessments;

    (iv) moving from place to place;

    (v) storing for hire or on a gratuitous bailment; and

    (vi) using, altering, and making repairs or alterations.

C. Stock and bond transactions. The language granting power with respect to stock and bond transactions empowers the agent to buy, sell, and exchange stocks, bonds, mutual funds, and all other types of securities and financial instruments except commodity futures contracts and call and put options on stocks and stock indexes, receive certificates and other evidences of ownership with respect to securities, exercise voting rights with respect to securities in person or by proxy, enter into voting trusts, and consent to limitations on the right to vote.

D. Commodity and option transactions. The language granting power with respect to commodity and option transactions empowers the agent to buy, sell, exchange, assign, settle, and exercise commodity futures contracts and call and put options on stocks and stock indexes traded on a regulated option exchange, and establish, continue, modify, and terminate option accounts with a broker.

E: Banking and other financial institution transactions. The language granting power with respect to banking and other financial institution transactions empowers the agent to:

(1) continue, modify, and terminate an account or other banking arrangement made by or on behalf of the principal;

(2) establish, modify, and terminate an account or other banking arrangement with a bank, trust company, savings and loan association, credit union, thrift company, brokerage firm, or other financial institution selected by the agent;

(3) hire a safe deposit box or space in a vault;

(4) contract to procure other services available from a financial institution as the agent considers desirable;

(5) withdraw by check, order, or otherwise money or property of the principal deposited with or left in the custody of a financial institution;

(6) receive bank statements, vouchers, notices, and similar documents from a financial institution and act with respect to them;

(7) enter a safe deposit box or vault and withdraw or add to the contents;

(8) borrow money at an interest rate agreeable to the agent and pledge as security personal property of the principal necessary in order to borrow, pay, renew, or extend the time of payment of a debt of the principal;

(9) make, assign, draw, endorse, discount, guarantee, and negotiate promissory notes, checks, drafts, and other negotiable or nonnegotiable paper of the principal, or payable to the principal or the principal's order, receive the cash or other proceeds of those transactions, accept a draft drawn by a person upon the principal, and pay it when due;

(10) receive for the principal and act upon a sight draft, warehouse receipt, or other negotiable or nonnegotiable instrument;

(11) apply for and receive letters of credit, credit cards, and traveler's checks from a financial institution, and give an indemnity or other agreement in connection with letters of credit; and (12) consent to an extension of the time of payment with respect to commercial paper or a financial transaction with a financial institution.

F. Business operating transactions. The language granting power with respect to business operating transactions empowers the agent to:

(1) operate, buy, sell, enlarge, reduce, and terminate a business interest;

(2) to the extent that an agent is permitted by law to act for a principal and subject to the terms of the partnership agreement to:

(i) perform a duty or discharge a liability and exercise a right, power, privilege, or option that the principal has, may have, or claims to have, under a partnership agreement, whether or not the principal is a partner;

(ii) enforce the terms of a partnership agreement by litigation or otherwise; and

(iii) defend, submit to arbitration, settle, or compromise litigation to which the principal is a party because of membership in the partnership;

(3) exercise in person or by proxy, or enforce by litigation or otherwise, a right, power, privilege, or option the principal has or claims to have as the holder of a bond, share, or other instrument of similar character and defend, submit to arbitration, settle, or compromise litigation to which the principal is a party because of a bond, share, or similar instrument;

(4) with respect to a business owned solely by the principal:

(i) continue, modify, renegotiate, extend, and terminate a contract made with an individual or a legal entity, firm, association, or corporation by or on behalf of the principal with respect to the business before execution of the power of attorney;

(ii) determine:

(A) the location of its operation;

(B) the nature and extent of its business;

(C) the methods of manufacturing, selling, merchandising, financing, accounting, and advertising employed in its operation;

(D) the amount and types of insurance carried;

(E) the mode of engaging, compensating, and dealing with its accountants, attorneys, and other agents and employees;

(iii) change the name or form of organization under which the business is operated and enter into a partnership agreement with other persons or organize a corporation to take over all or part of the operation of the business; and

(iv) demand and receive money due or claimed by the principal or on the principal's behalf in the operation of the business, and control and disburse the money in the operation of the business;

(5) put additional capital into a business in which the principal has an interest;

(6) join in a plan of reorganization, consolidation, or merger of the business;

(7) sell or liquidate a business or part of it at the time and upon the terms the agent considers desirable;

(8) establish the value of a business under a buy-out agreement to which the principal is a party;

(9) prepare, sign, file, and deliver reports, compilations of information, returns, or other papers with respect to a business which are required by a governmental agency or instrumentality or which the agent considers desirable, and make related payments; and

(10) pay, compromise, or contest taxes or assessments and do any other act which the agent considers desirable to protect the principal from illegal or unnecessary taxation, fines, penalties, or assessments with respect to a business, including attempts to recover, in any manner permitted by law, money paid before or after the execution of the power of attorney.

G. Insurance and annuity transactions. The language granting power with respect to insurance and annuity transactions empowers the agent to:

(1) continue, pay the premium or assessment on, modify, rescind, release, or terminate a contract procured by or on behalf of the principal which insures or provides an annuity to either the principal or another person, whether or not the principal is a beneficiary under the contract;

(2) procure new, different, and additional contracts of insurance and annuities for the principal and the principal's spouse, children, and other dependents; and select the amount, type of insurance or annuity, and mode of payment;

(3) pay the premium or assessment on, modify, rescind, release, or terminate a contract of insurance or annuity procured by the agent;

(4) designate the beneficiary of the contract, but an agent may be named a beneficiary of the contract, or an extension, renewal, or substitute for it, only to the extent the agent was named as a beneficiary under a contract procured by the principal before executing the power of attorney;

(5) apply for and receive a loan on the security of the contract of insurance or annuity;

(6) surrender and receive the cash surrender value;

(7) exercise an election;

(8) change the manner of paying premiums;

(9) change or convert the type of insurance contract or annuity, with respect to which the principal has or claims to have a power described in this section;

(10) change the beneficiary of a contract of insurance or annuity, but the agent may not be designated a beneficiary except to the extent permitted by paragraph (4);

(11) apply for and procure government aid to guarantee or pay premiums of a contract of insurance on the life of the principal;

(12) collect, sell, assign, hypothecate, borrow upon, or pledge the interest of the principal in a contract of insurance or annuity; and

(13) pay from proceeds or otherwise, compromise or contest, and apply for refunds in connection with, a tax or assessment levied by a taxing authority with respect to a contract of insurance or annuity or its proceeds or liability accruing by reason of the tax or assessment.

H. Estate, trust, and other beneficiary transactions. The language granting power with respect to estate, trust, and other beneficiary transactions, empowers the agent to act for the principal in all matters that affect a trust, probate estate, guardianship, conservatorship, escrow, custodianship, or other fund from which the principal is, may become, or claims to be entitled, as a beneficiary, to a share or payment, including to:

(1) accept, reject, disclaim, receive, receipt for, sell, assign, release, pledge, exchange, or consent to a reduction in or modification of a share in or payment from the fund;

(2) demand or obtain by litigation or otherwise money or other thing of value to which the principal is, may become, or claims to be entitled by reason of the fund;

(3) initiate, participate in, and oppose litigation to ascertain the meaning, validity, or effect of a deed, will, declaration of trust, or other instrument or transaction affecting the interest of the principal;

(4) initiate, participate in, and oppose litigation to remove, substitute, or surcharge a fiduciary;

(5) conserve, invest, disburse, and use anything received for an authorized purpose; and

(6) transfer an interest of the principal in real property, stocks, bonds, accounts with financial institutions, insurance, and other property, to the trustee of a revocable trust created by the principal as settlor.

I. Claims and litigation. The language granting power with respect to claims and litigation empowers the agent to:

(1) assert and prosecute before a court or administrative agency a claim, a [claim for relief] [cause of action], counterclaim, offset, and defend against an individual, a legal entity, or government, including suits to recover property or other thing of value, to recover damages sustained by the principal, to eliminate or modify tax liability, or to seek an injunction, specific performance, or other relief;

(2) bring an action to determine adverse claims, intervene in litigation, and act as amicus curiae;

(3) in connection with litigation, procure an attachment, garnishment, libel, order of arrest, or other preliminary, provisional, or intermediate relief and use an available procedure to effect or satisfy a judgment, order, or decree;

(4) in connection with litigation, perform any lawful act, including acceptance of tender, offer of judgment, admission of facts, submission of a controversy on an agreed statement of facts, consent to examination before trial, and binding the principal in litigation;

(5) submit to arbitration, settle, and propose or accept a compromise with respect to a claim or litigation;

(6) waive the issuance and service of process upon the principal, accept service of process, appear for the principal, designate persons upon whom process directed to the principal may be served, execute and file or deliver stipulations on the principal's behalf, verify pleadings, seek appellate review, procure and give surety and indemnity bonds, contract and pay for the preparation and printing of records and briefs, receive and execute and file or deliver a consent, waiver, release, confession of judgment, satisfaction of judgment, notice, agreement, or other instrument in connection with the prosecution, settlement, or defense of a claim or litigation;

(7) act for the principal with respect to bankruptcy or insolvency proceedings, whether voluntary or involuntary, concerning the principal or some other person, with respect to a reorganization proceeding, or a receivership or application for the appointment of a receiver or trustee which affects an interest of the principal in property or other thing of value; and

(8) pay a judgment against the principal or a settlement made in connection with litigation and receive and conserve money, or other thing of value paid in settlement of or as proceeds of a claim or litigation.

J. Personal and family maintenance. The language granting power with respect to personal and family maintenance empowers the agent to:

(1) do the acts necessary to maintain the customary standard of living of the principal, the principal's spouse, children, and other individuals customarily or legally entitled to be supported by the principal, including providing living quarters by purchase, lease, or other contract, or paying the operating costs, including interest, amortization payments, repairs, and taxes on premises owned by the principal and occupied by those individuals;

(2) provide for the individuals described in paragraph (1) normal domestic help; usual vacations and travel expenses; and funds for shelter, clothing, food, appropriate education, and other current living costs;

(3) pay for the individuals described in paragraph (1) necessary medical, dental, and surgical care, hospitalization, and custodial care;

(4) continue any provision made by the principal, for the individuals described in paragraph (1), for automobiles or other means of transportation, including registering, licensing, insuring, and replacing them;

(5) maintain or open charge accounts for the convenience of the individuals described in paragraph (1) and open new accounts the agent considers desirable to accomplish a lawful purpose; and

(6) continue payments incidental to the membership or affiliation of the principal in a church, club, society, order, or other organization or to continue contributions to those organizations.

K. Benefits from social security, medicare, medicaid, or other governmental programs, or military service. The language granting power with respect to benefits from social security, medicare, Medicaid, or other governmental programs, or military service empowers the agent to:

(1) execute vouchers in the name of the principal for allowances and reimbursements payable by the United States or a foreign government or by a state or subdivision of a state to the principal, including allowances and reimbursements for transportation of the individuals described in Section 13(1), and for shipment of their household effects;

(2) take possession and order the removal and shipment of property of the principal from a post, warehouse, depot, dock, or other place of storage or safekeeping, either governmental or private, and execute and deliver a release, voucher, receipt, bill of lading, shipping ticket, certificate, or other instrument for that purpose;

(3) prepare, file, and prosecute a claim of the principal to a benefit or assistance, financial or otherwise, to which the principal claims to be entitled, under a statute or governmental regulation;

(4) prosecute, defend, submit to arbitration, settle, and propose or accept a compromise with respect to any benefits the principal may be entitled to receive; and

(5) receive the financial proceeds of a claim of the type described in this section, conserve, invest, disburse, or use anything received for a lawful purpose.

L. Retirement plan transactions. The language granting power with respect to retirement plan transactions empowers the agent to:

(1) select payment options under any retirement plan in which the principal participates, including plans for self-employed individuals;

(2) designate beneficiaries under those plans and change existing designations;

(3) make voluntary contributions to those plans;

(4) exercise the investment powers available under any self-directed retirement plan;

(5) make "rollovers" of plan benefits into other retirement plans;

(6) if authorized by the plan, borrow from, sell assets to, and purchase assets from the plan; and

(7) waive the right of the principal to be a beneficiary of a joint or survivor annuity if the principal is a spouse who is not employed.

M. Tax matters. The language granting power with respect to tax matters empowers the agent to:

(1) prepare, sign, and file federal, state, local, and foreign income, gift, payroll, Federal Insurance Contributions Act returns, and other tax returns, claims for refunds, requests for extension of time, petitions regarding tax matters, and any other tax-related documents, including receipts, offers, waivers, consents (including consents and agreements under Internal Revenue Code Section 2032A or any successor section), closing agreements, and any power of attorney required by the Internal Revenue Service or other taxing authority with respect to a tax year upon which the statute of limitations has not run and the following 25 tax years;

(2) pay taxes due, collect refunds, post bonds, receive confidential information, and contest deficiencies determined by the Internal Revenue Service or other taxing authority;

(3) exercise any election available to the principal under federal, state, local, or foreign tax law; and

(4) act for the principal in all tax matters for all periods before the Internal Revenue Service, and any other taxing authority.

Form derived from Uniform Statutory Form Power of Attorney Act, NCCUSL©1989, with permission.

A Conversation about Financial Powers of Attorney

Client:
What can I do to increase the likelihood that my bank and stockbroker will honor my Power of Attorney and let my agent manage my money?

Lawyer:
Take copies of your document to your banker, broker, and any other representatives of the institutions where you do business to see if it is acceptable to them. Be sure to do this soon after creating it—before you become disabled. If your financial institutions have a problem with the Power of Attorney form you have executed, you need to execute one that is acceptable to them—perhaps their own form.

Client:
Does this mean I might have several Powers of Attorney? I'm not sure that makes sense.

Lawyer:
It is okay to give your agent a general Financial Power of Attorney (like the one provided in this book), and also give him or her a specific Power of Attorney created by your bank or brokerage house. As long as the multiple Powers of Attorney appoint the same agent, no problems arise.

Client:
Once I have taken care of that, what should I do with my Power of Attorney?

Lawyer:
Choosing where to keep it should be carefully considered because the document becomes effective as soon as it is signed. As soon as your agent comes into possession of the original form, he or she may exercise any and all powers you have granted.

Your form should only be stored in your safe deposit box if you have authorized the bank to allow your agent access to the box. A better choice is a strongbox at home or the office, or a similar safe place that is reasonably accessible to your agent. Be sure that your agent knows where it can be found.

Client:

I have heard it is a good idea to do a new Power of Attorney every so often, but I am not sure what "often" means.

Lawyer:

Financial institutions do prefer to honor Powers of Attorney that have been executed fairly recently, as that leaves less time for you to have revoked it. A rule of thumb is to create a new Power of Attorney form every five years *if the agent is the same.* Obviously, you would do a new form if your agent changed for any reason.

Client:

Given the range of my financial affairs, should I fine-tune my Power of Attorney form? For example, should I not hold back access to my stock accounts or some other type of property?

Lawyer:

The specific powers your grant are your decision. The form has space to list powers that you want to deny your agent. However, it is probably best to give your agent as broad a grant of powers as possible because you have no way of anticipating every future situation. For example, Jane limits her agent's ability to sell her collection of commemorative plates. However, a time comes when the agent either has to sell a piece of real estate in a depressed market or sell the collection to pay for Jane's long-term care. He may know that if she able to decide, Jane would choose the latter because, over the long run, the property would increase in value more than the plates. This would be relevant if she were also concerned with leaving some estate for her children.

Instructions for Completing the Draft Power of Attorney Form

Gather the following information:

1. Your name.
2. Your city and state.
3. Your agent's name.
4. Your agent's city and state.
5. All of the powers you want to give your agent.
   a. If you want to give your agent complete power over all of your financial affairs, place your initials before the letter N *or* place your initials before every letter, from A to N.
   b. If you want to give your agent power over some, but not all of your financial affairs, place your initials before the letters listing the powers you want to give your agent. For example, if you do not want your agent to be able to sell your real estate, but want to give your agent power over the rest of your finances, place your initials before every letter but the letter A, which is the power over real property transactions. You could also cross out the "real property transactions" power. You could also do both—initial the line before letters B-N as well as crossing out line A, "real property transactions."
6. Any special instructions you want to give your agent. For example, you may want to tell your agent to pay your mother's medical bills.

   NOTE: *You do not have to fill out this section.*

7. The date you will sign your Power of Attorney.
8. Your Social Security number.

Do not sign the draft. Go to Chapter 6, "Preparing and Signing your Will, Living Will, and Power of Attorney."

Draft

Power of Attorney

I (1)_____ of (2)_____, _____
appoint (3)_____ of (4)_____, _____
as my agent to act for me in any lawful way with respect to the following initialed subjects:

TO GRANT ALL OF THE FOLLOWING POWERS, INITIAL THE LINE IN FRONT OF (N) AND IGNORE THE LINES IN FRONT OF THE OTHER POWERS.

TO GRANT ONE OR MORE, BUT FEWER THAN ALL, OF THE FOLLOWING POWERS, INITIAL THE LINE IN FRONT OF EACH POWER YOU ARE GRANTING.

TO WITHHOLD A POWER, DO NOT INITIAL THE LINE IN FRONT OF IT. YOU MAY, BUT NEED NOT, CROSS OUT EACH POWER WITHHELD.

(5) INITIAL

_____ (A)   Real property transactions.

_____ (B)   Tangible personal property transactions.

_____ (C)   Stock and bond transactions.

_____ (D)   Commodity and option transactions.

_____ (E)   Banking and other financial institution transactions.

_____ (F)   Business operating transactions.

_____ (G)   Insurance and annuity transactions.

_____ (H)   Estate, trust, and other beneficiary transactions.

_____ (I)   Claims and litigation.

_____ (J)   Personal and family maintenance.

_____ (K)   Benefits from Social Security, Medicare, Medicaid, or other governmental programs, or military service.

_____ (L)   Retirement plan transactions.

_____ (M)   Tax matters.

_____ (N)   ALL OF THE POWERS LISTED ABOVE. YOU NEED NOT INITIAL ANY OTHER LINES IF YOU INITIAL LINE (N).

ON THE FOLLOWING LINES YOU MAY GIVE SPECIAL INSTRUCTIONS LIMITING OR EXTENDING THE POWERS GRANTED TO YOUR AGENT.

(6)_____

_____

_____

UNLESS YOU DIRECT OTHERWISE ABOVE, THIS POWER OF ATTORNEY IS EFFECTIVE IMMEDIATELY AND WILL CONTINUE UNTIL IT IS REVOKED.

This power of attorney will continue to be effective even though I become disabled, incapacitated, or incompetent.

I agree that any third party who receives a copy of this document may act under it. Revocation of the power of attorney is not effective as to a third party until the third party learns of the revocation. I agree to indemnify the third party for any claims that arise against the third party because of reliance on this power of attorney.

Signed this (7)_____ day of _____, 20_____.

_____

[Signature]

(8)_____

[Social Security Number]

WITNESSES:

_____ _____

[Signature of Witness]   [Signature of Witness]

_____ _____

[Name]   [Name]

_____ _____

[Address]   [Address]

State of _____)

County of _____)

This document was acknowledged before me on _____ by

_____,   _____,   _____,

[Name of Principal]   [Name of Witness]   [Name of Witness]

_____

[Signature of Notarial Officer]

[Seal, if any]

_____

[Title (and Rank)]

My commission expires: _____

BY ACCEPTING OR ACTING UNDER THE APPOINTMENT, THE AGENT ASSUMES THE FIDUCIARY AND OTHER LEGAL RESPONSIBILITIES OF AN AGENT.

Form derived from Uniform Statutory Form Power of Attorney Act, NCCUSL©1989, with permission.

NOTE: *You will attach the list of the definitions to your final form, but they are omitted here.*

Chapter 6:
Preparing and Signing Your Final Documents

At this point, you deserve a pat on the back. You have made the important decision to protect yourself and your loved ones, and you have gathered the information and performed the tasks to make that possible. You now have only to prepare your final documents in order to have a valid Will, Health Care Advance Directive, and Power of Attorney. This chapter guides you through that process step by step.

> **Caution:** This is *not* the time be get careless! What may seem trivial— one erased word, one unnumbered page—may invite questions about the validity of your documents. All your planning may be for naught if minor errors creep into your final Will and other documents. Be sure to attend to the details.

Preparing Your Final Will

Your final Will—the one you will sign—must be completely type written or word-processed. You cannot just fill in the blanks of your correct form. You need to completely retype the form, leaving no blank spaces. There should be no erasures or whiteouts. What you want to avoid is any suspicion that you or anyone else changed the Will after it was signed. Remember, it may be decades before your Will is probated. If it has blank spaces at the signing, it is easy for someone during those decades to fill in blank spaces, or make corrections with whiteout or an eraser, and change who gets your property. Courts suspect blank spaces, erasures, and white outs. You also do not want handwritten or typed corrections or cross-outs in your final Will. Do not add anything handwritten to your completed Will—before or after signing. These shortcuts invite court disputes.

Executing Your Final Will and Self-Proving Affidavit

Lawyers refer to the act of signing your Will as *executing* your Will. Executing your Will is a serious undertaking. If it is not done correctly, you die without a valid Will—leaving you with a Will that has no legal effect. Your property goes to your intestate heirs, determined by the laws of your state.

The legal formalities you must follow to correctly execute your Will include the following.

◆ You should gather your witnesses and a notary (for the Self-Proving Affidavit) together in a private room free from distractions. The Will forms call for three witnesses (although you only need two witnesses in all states except Vermont). It is usually no more trouble to gather three than two, and if there is a need for a live witness years later, you have an additional person to call. Your witnesses must be 18 years old. Your witnesses must NOT inherit from the Will, or be named as executor, trustee, or guardian. Your witnesses must be disinterested in the outcome of the Will.

◆ You should say to your witnesses:

This is my Will. I have read it, understand it, and it contains my wishes. I want you three people to be my witnesses.

Your witnesses do not need to read your Will. They do not need to know your wishes. They *do* need to know that the document they are witnessing you sign is your Will.

◆ You, in the presence of all witnesses and the notary, should date and sign your name at the end of the Will and Self-Proving Affidavit and initial every page. Your signature should be exactly as what your name is printed in the Will.

◆ Write your name and the name of your witnesses in the blank spaces indicated in the Self-Proving Affidavit.

◆ You and your witnesses must watch as each witness signs your Will and Self-Proving Affidavit in ink, and initials each page of your Will and affidavit. The witnesses should write their addresses in the space indicated. Their addresses are not legally necessary but can help if someone needs to track them down years from now.

NOTE: *See page 72 for an example of how the witness signatures should be completed.*

- ◆ You should give the Self-Proving Affidavit to the notary for execution.
- ◆ The notary will administer an oath and have you and the witnesses swear to the truth of the statements in the affidavit. The notary might require identification (typically a driver's license) from you and your witnesses. The notary will sign, seal, and date the affidavit.
- ◆ You should make sure that you have paginated the entire Will and Self-Proving Affidavit.
- ◆ You should staple together the Will and Self-Proving Affidavit.

Preparing Your Final Health Care Advance Directive and Power of Attorney

Your final Health Care Advance Directive and Power of Attorney can be used right out of the Appendix. You can fill in the blanks of these forms as you filled in the blanks of your draft form. You can photocopy or retype these forms, or you can use the CD-ROM to create your own.

Signing Your Final Health Care Advance Directive and Power of Attorney

After you have executed your Will, you and your witnesses should sign the directive and Power of Attorney. Obtain the notary's acknowledgment.

At this point, you should have a valid Will, Health Care Advance Directive, and Power of Attorney. Congratulations! The next—and final chapter, offers tips on storing these important documents in a safe place, as well as other additional information.

Chapter 7:
Storing, Revoking, or Changing Your Will

Now that you have a valid Will, Health Care Advance Directive, and Power of Attorney, it is important that you store them in an appropriate place. You want them to be safe, but you also want to ensure that they can be placed in the right hands when they are needed. This chapter offers tips on storing these documents, as well as information about updating them whenever necessary.

Your Will

The most important point to remember when storing your Will is this: *Only the original Will can be presented for probate.* You will need copies, but they will be for information purposes only. Take care to store your Will and other important papers in a fireproof strongbox is likely to be the most practical idea. Remember, your executor would not have access to your safe deposit box unless you have specified so. Furthermore, some states require banks to seal the deceased's safe deposit box until the state taxing authority does an inventory of the contents. This could delay your executor getting started on your Will. Some states allow you to file your Will for safekeeping with the court.

Originals vs. Copies of Your Will

You should have just one signed original of your Will. Some people think it will be helpful to have *duplicate originals*, in which more than one original, signed Will would exist. This can cause problems at probate. But you should make copies of your Will for later review. Give a copy to your executor, with instructions for locating your original Will. Giving copies of your Will to your beneficiaries is purely a personal—not a legal decision.

Revoking Your Will

The most common and effective way to revoke your Will is to make a new Will that states you revoke all prior Wills. Every Will form in this book contains a statement revoking all prior Wills. Problems can arise by other methods of revocation. Just turning your Will into ashes may not be enough in all states. Destruction must be combined with intent to destroy in order to legally revoke your Will. This intent to destroy can be difficult to prove after your death, especially if copies of your burned Will are produced at probate. It is much easier to have a new Will that expressly revokes any and all earlier Wills.

When to Make a New Will

Many life events can call for a new Will. The most frequent reasons people make a new Will include:

- marriage or divorce;
- having more children, either biological or adopted;
- significant increases or decreases in wealth;
- death of a beneficiary;
- changing opinions about who should receive property;
- death of a child, leaving grandchildren or stepchildren; or,
- appointed executor, trustee, or guardian is no longer suitable.

NOTE: *Never make any changes on your final Will! This could invalidate the entire Will. As a result, you may die without a Will and your intestate heirs will inherit your property.*

Your Health Care Advance Directive

Unlike your Will and Power of Attorney, presenting your original Health Care Directive document usually is not critical to its use. What is most important is to have copies of the directive in the hands of those—particularly your named agent—who will need to make medical decisions when you are unable to make them for yourself.

What to Do with Your Directive

You will want to give your directive to your agent once it is completed. It should be kept in a safe place, of course, but it should be accessible. This is one document in which the contents should already be familiar, as you will have discussed your wishes with your agent (usually your spouse). Make as many copies as you need to ensure that those with a role in your medical treatment and care are well informed about your wishes—physicians, health care facility, close family members, etc. Should you need care in a new facility, be sure to provide a copy at the time of admission.

Revoking or Changing Your Directive

As you have named a health care agent and two alternates, and you have carefully thought through your wishes, you may not need to ever change your directive. However, you have the right to revoke (take away) your agent's authority at any time. To do so, notify your agent and all those with copies of your document. Destroy the original, and make a new directive as soon as possible.

When to Make a New Directive

As with other documents, there are times when preparing a new directive is wise, including:

- ◆ death of agent or alternates;
- ◆ marriage or divorce; and,
- ◆ change in your wishes about care.

Your Power of Attorney

It is critical that you remember this about your Power of Attorney—*once signed, the document is effective (useable).* Unlike a Will, which must be presented for probate and proven to be valid by the court, the original Power of Attorney can be used by your agent to get to your money in your bank or other financial institution. However, while you should be aware of this fact and keep it in mind should something change in your relationship with your agent, the person that you have selected should have only been selected at all because it is someone in which you have complete trust.

Where to Store Your Power of Attorney

As with your Will, a fireproof strongbox is likely to be the best option for storing your Power of Attorney, since your agent would not have access to your safe deposit box. Since this document can be used from the moment it is signed, it is a good idea for you to keep it safely stored, but accessible to your agent when it is needed. An alternative to the strongbox is the safe deposit box if your agent has access to it, or another safe place known to your agent.

Originals vs. Copies of the Power of Attorney

Again, the original document should be well protected. You may wish to give a copy to your agent and your bank, for *information only*. As financial institutions sometimes prefer their own forms, you may have *more than one* Power of Attorney to safeguard. As stated, any Power of Attorney becomes effective as soon as you sign it, but your agent *must have* the signed, notarized form before he or she can act on your behalf.

Revoking or Changing Your Power of Attorney

You name only one agent—no alternates—so you will need to make a new Power of Attorney if your designated agent dies or becomes unavailable. You should be aware that financial institutions may be more suspicious about an old Power of Attorney, as much time may have passed since your wishes were stated (thus giving more time for alterations to have been made). Therefore, it is a good idea to make a new Power of Attorney every five years, even if there are no changes.

If you want to revoke your Power of Attorney, and it has never left your possession, just tear it up. If you have given a copy to your bank, you must notify officials in writing that you are revoking it. Remember that this document must conform to state law, so when you prepare it, be sure to ask about revocation procedures.

When to Make a New Power of Attorney

As you have named only one agent, you must make a new Power of Attorney if that person dies; is incapacitated; or, is otherwise unable to manage your financial affairs on your behalf. Since you are likely to have named your spouse or close relative as agent, these situations may call for a new Power of Attorney:

- events have made you think your agent is no longer suitable;
- death of agent;
- major change in financial situation; or,
- provisions are no longer up-to-date.

Glossary

A

administrator. A person the probate court appoints to manage and distribute the estate of a person who has died without a Will.

agent. The person you appoint to act for you.

B

beneficiary. The person named in a Will to receive money or property.

bequeath. The act of making a gift to someone.

bequest. A gift made in the Will.

bond. An insurance policy required by a court that protects against the possibility of fraud or embezzlement by a trustee or an executor. The Will-maker may request in the Will that no bond be required.

C

Children's Trust. A trust set up as part of a Will or outside of a Will to provide funds for a child.

codicil. An addition or supplement to a Will. It must be executed with the same procedures as a Will.

creditor. Someone who has a right to require the fulfillment of an obligation or contract.

custodian. The person appointed to manage and dispense funds for a child without court supervision and accounting requirements.

D

decedent. A person who has died.

descendant. Those who have issued from an individual, including children, grandchildren, and their children, through the generations.

durable power of attorney. Unlike ordinary Powers of Attorney, durable powers can survive for long periods of time, and again, unlike standard Powers of Attorney, durable powers can continue after incompetency.

E

estate. A term commonly used to denote the sum total of all types of property owned by a person at a particular time, usually upon his or her death.

executor. The person or entity named in a Will who has the responsibility of carrying out the terms of the Will.

G

general power of attorney. A document under which a grantor gives an agent wide-ranging powers to act on behalf of the grantor.

H

health care advance directive. A document that combines instructions about your health care should you be unable to speak for yourself and the Power of Attorney to make health care decisions for you. *See living will.*

health care power of attorney. A document that designates someone to make health care decisions for someone else if that person is incompetent to make such decisions.

I

indemnity. An agreement whereby one party agrees to secure another against an anticipated loss or damage.

inherit. The act of receiving property from a decedent's estate.

intestate. A person who dies without a Will is said to die "intestate."

intestate succession. This refers to the law of the state providing for the inheritance of property from a person who dies without leaving a Will.

J

joint tenancy. A method by which one person mutually holds legal title to property with other persons in such a way that, in most states, when one of the joint owners dies his or her share automatically passes to the surviving joint owners by operation of law.

L

legacy. A gift of money or of personal property where the title is passed under the terms of a Will.

legal will. A Will made in accordance with your state's law, signed, and witnessed.

lineal descendant. This includes all persons who come from your loins (children, grandchildren, great grandchildren, etc.).

living trust. A trust created during the maker's lifetime.

living will. Directions telling what health care you wish if you cannot make health care decisions yourself.

M

minor. A person who does not have the legal rights of an adult. A minor is usually defined as someone who has not yet reached the age of majority; in most states, a person reaches majority and acquires all of the rights and responsibilities of an adult when he or she turns age 18.

N

notary public. A notary public is a public official who, depending on the state, has the power to acknowledge signatures, administer oaths and affirmations, take depositions, and issue subpoenas in lawsuits.

P

pay on death (POD). These are specific directions to give someone property (usually bank accounts or securities) at your death.

property. The sum of all things and money you own.

probate. The process of gathering the decedent's assets, winding up the decedents financial affairs, and distributing the remainder to heirs or beneficiaries.

R

remainder. Balance of any property in an estate distributed to heirs or beneficiaries.

right of survivorship. Property automatically goes to the co-owners if one of the co-owners dies.

S

securities. An investment in an enterprise with the expectation of profit from the efforts of other people; for example, any note, stock certificate, bond, debenture, check, etc.

self-proving will. A Will having an attached affidavit signed by a notary public that shows the Will was properly signed and witnessed and that it is the Will of the person who signed it.

specific legacy. A bequest of a particular thing to a specific person.

successor trustee. One who follows or comes into the place of another.

surviving spouse. The wife or husband who lives after the person who made the Will.

T

tenancy in common. A type of joint ownership that allows a person to sell his or her share or leave it in a Will without the consent of the other owners.

termination date. The date at which a testator desires a young person to receive a bequest.

testate. A person who dies with a valid Will.

testator. One who has made a testament or Will.

trust. Property given to a trustee to manage for the benefit of a third person.

W

will. The legal declaration of a person's intentions of what he or she Wills to be performed after his or her death.

witness. One who is called upon to be present at a transaction, as the making of a Will.

Appendix:
Blank Forms

This appendix contains all the forms discussed throughout the text. You can use these blank forms by removing them along their perforated edge or downloading them from the attached CD-ROM. (See "How to Use the CD-ROM" on page xi.)

If you do use the blank forms attached in the book, photocopy them first so that if you make a mistake, wish to change something prior to executing your document, or wish to make changes in the future, you have an unmarked form to use.

Table of Forms

WILL
Married with Adult Children

Will of _____

I, _____ of _____,
make this my Will. I revoke any other Wills and codicils made by me.

1. Family

I am married to _____, my spouse. I have _____
children, _____, my children. The term
"my children" includes the aforementioned children, all children born after the making of this Will,
and all children adopted by me.

2. Residuary Estate

A. I give my residuary estate, that is, all of my property, real, personal, and mixed, of whatever kind and wherever situated, of which I may die possessed, to my spouse, _____, if my spouse survives me.

B. If my spouse does not survive me, I leave this residuary estate, in equal shares, to my children.

C. If a child does not survive me, then the deceased child's share devolves, in equal shares, to the deceased child's children. If none of the deceased child's children survive me, then this share devolves, in equal shares, to my surviving children.

D. If a deceased child's children are entitled to a share of my estate, I leave this bequest to my trustee to be held in trust under Article 4, "Grandchild's Trust."

3. Appointment of Fiduciaries

A. Executor. I appoint my spouse to serve as my executor. If my spouse cannot serve, then I appoint _____ to serve as my executor.

B. Trustee. I appoint _____ to serve as my trustee. If _____ cannot serve, then I appoint _____ to serve as my trustee.

C. No bond shall be required of my executor or trustee.

4. Grandchild's Trust

My trustee shall hold the assets passing to my grandchildren in a separate trust for each grandchild under this article until that grandchild has reached the age of _____ years, the termination date.

Initials: _____ _____ _____ _____   Page _____ of _____
         Testator   Witness   Witness   Witness

A. Until the termination date, my trustee shall distribute to or for the benefit of my grandchild as much of the net income and principal as my trustee may consider appropriate for the grandchild's health, education, support, or maintenance, annually adding to principal any undistributed income.

B. Upon the termination date, my trustee shall distribute the remaining assets to the grandchild.

5. Miscellaneous

My executor and trustee shall exercise all powers conferred by law, in addition to the following powers, which are to be exercised in the best interest of my estate or trust.

A. To hold and retain any property owned by me.

B. To sell, exchange, or lease any property.

C. To vote stock; to convert securities belonging to my estate into other securities; and, to exercise all other rights and privileges of a person owning similar properties.

D. To settle claims.

E. To pay all debts and taxes.

F. To do all other acts necessary for the proper management, investment, and distribution of my estate or trust.

G. To take all actions to have the probate of this Will conducted as free of court supervision as possible.

I have signed this Will in the presence of the undersigned witnesses on this _____ day of _____, 20_____, at _____, State of _____, and declare it is my Will, that I signed it willingly, that I executed it as my free and voluntary act for the purpose expressed herein, and that I am of legal age and sound mind.

_____

[Signature]

The foregoing instrument was on said date subscribed at the end thereof by _____, the above named testator who signed, published, and declared this instrument to be his/her Last Will and Testament in the presence of us and each of us, who thereupon at his/her request, in his/her presence, and in the presence of each other, have hereunto subscribed our names as witnesses thereto. We are of sound mind and proper age to witness a will and understand this to be his/her will, and to the best of our knowledge testator is of legal age to make a will, of sound mind, and under no constraint or undue influence.

_____ residing at _____

_____ residing at _____

_____ residing at _____

WILL
Married with Young Children

Will of _____

I, _____ of _____,
make this my Will. I revoke any other Wills and codicils made by me.

1. Family

I am married to _____, my spouse. I have _____
children, _____, my children. The term
"my children" includes the aforementioned children, all children born after the making of this Will,
and all children adopted by me.

2. Residuary Estate

A. I give my residuary estate, that is, all of my property, real, personal, and mixed, of whatever kind and wherever situated, of which I may die possessed, to my spouse,
_____, if my spouse survives me.

B. If my spouse does not survive me, I leave this residuary estate to my children. If my
youngest child has, on the date of my death, reached the age of _____ years, I leave this
residuary estate outright to my children, in equal shares. If my youngest child has not,
on the date of my death, reached the age of _____ years, I leave this residuary estate to
my trustee to be held in trust under Article 4, "Children's Trust."

C   If a child does not survive me and no "Children's Trust" is created according to Article 2.B
above, then the deceased child's share devolves, in equal shares, to the deceased child's children. If none of the deceased child's children survive me, then this share devolves, in equal
shares, to my surviving children.

D. If a deceased child's children are entitled to a share of my estate, I leave this bequest to
my trustee to be held in trust under Article 5, "Grandchild's Trust."

3. Appointment of Fiduciaries

A. Executor. I appoint my spouse to serve as my executor. If my spouse cannot serve, then
I appoint _____ to serve as my executor.

B. Guardian. If, at my death, any of my children are minors and a guardian is needed for my minor children, I appoint _____ to serve as my guardian. If _____ cannot serve, then I appoint _____ to serve as my guardian.

C. Trustee. I appoint _____ to serve as my trustee. If _____ cannot serve, then I appoint _____ to serve as my trustee.

D. No bond shall be required of my executor, trustee, or guardian.

4. Children's Trust

If a "Children's Trust" is created according to Article 2.B above, my trustee shall hold the assets passing to my children in trust under this article.

A. Until the termination date, my trustee shall distribute to or for the benefit of my children as much of the net income and principal as my trustee may consider appropriate for their health, education, support, or maintenance, annually adding to principal any undistributed income. My trustee may distribute income and principal unequally, and may distribute to some children and not to others. My trustee may consider other income and assets readily available to my children in making distributions.

B. Upon the termination date, my trustee shall distribute the remaining assets, in equal shares, to my surviving children.

C. The termination date is the date on which my youngest living child reaches the age of _____ years.

5. Grandchild's Trust

My trustee shall hold the assets passing to my grandchildren in a separate trust for each grandchild under this article until that grandchild has reached the age of _____ years, the termination date.

A. Until the termination date, my trustee shall distribute to or for the benefit of my grandchild as much of the net income and principal as my trustee may consider appropriate for the grandchild's health, education, support, or maintenance, annually adding to principal any undistributed income.

B. Upon the termination date, my trustee shall distribute the remaining assets to the grandchild.

6. Miscellaneous

My executor and trustee shall exercise all powers conferred by law, in addition to the following powers, which are to be exercised in the best interest of my estate or trust.

    A. To hold and retain any property owned by me.

    B. To sell, exchange, or lease any property.

    C. To vote stock; to convert securities belonging to my estate into other securities; and, to exercise all other rights and privileges of a person owning similar properties.

    D. To settle claims.

    E. To pay all debts and taxes.

    F. To do all other acts necessary for the proper management, investment, and distribution of my estate or trust.

    G. To take all actions to have the probate of this Will conducted as free of court supervision as possible.

I have signed this Will in the presence of the undersigned witnesses on this _____ day of _____, 20_____, at _____, State of _____, and declare it is my Will, that I signed it willingly, that I executed it as my free and voluntary act for the purpose expressed herein, and that I am of legal age and sound mind.

_____

[Signature]

The foregoing instrument was on said date subscribed at the end thereof by _____, the above named testator who signed, published, and declared this instrument to be his/her Last Will and Testament in the presence of us and each of us, who thereupon at his/her request, in his/her presence, and in the presence of each other, have hereunto subscribed our names as witnesses thereto. We are of sound mind and proper age to witness a will and understand this to be his/her will, and to the best of our knowledge testator is of legal age to make a will, of sound mind, and under no constraint or undue influence.

_____ residing at _____
_____ residing at _____
_____ residing at _____

This page intentionally blank.

WILL
Married without Children

Will of _____

I, _____ of _____, make this my Will. I revoke any other wills and codicils made by me.

1. Family

I am married to _____.

2. Residuary Estate

A. I give my residuary estate, that is, all of my property, real, personal, and mixed, of whatever kind and wherever situated, of which I may die possessed, to my spouse, _____, if my spouse survives me.

B. If my spouse does not survive me, I leave my residuary estate to the following:

1. _____
   _____

2. _____
   _____

3. _____
   _____
   _____
   _____

3. Appointment of Fiduciaries

A. Executor. I appoint my spouse to serve as my executor. If my spouse cannot serve, then I appoint _____ to serve as my executor.

B. Trustee. I appoint _____ to serve as my trustee. If _____ cannot serve, then I appoint _____ to serve as my trustee.

C. No bond shall be required of my executor, or trustee.

4. Young Person's Trust

My trustee shall hold the assets passing to young persons in a separate trust for each young person under this article until that young person has reached the age of _____ years, the termination date.

A. Until the termination date, my trustee shall distribute to or for the benefit of the young person as much of the net income and principal as my trustee may consider appropriate for the young person's health, education, support, or maintenance, annually adding to principal any undistributed income.

B. Upon the termination date, my trustee shall distribute the remaining assets to the young person.

5. Miscellaneous

My executor shall exercise all powers conferred by law, in addition to the following powers, which are to be exercised in the best interest of my estate or trust.

A. To hold and retain any property owned by me.

B. To sell, exchange, or lease any property.

C. To vote stock; to convert securities belonging to my estate into other securities; and, to exercise all other rights and privileges of a person owning similar properties.

D. To settle claims.

E. To pay all debts and taxes.

F. To do all other acts necessary for the proper management, investment, and distribution of my estate or trust.

G. To take all actions to have the probate of this Will conducted as free of court supervision as possible.

I have signed this Will in the presence of the undersigned witnesses on this _____ day of _____, 20_____, at _____, State of _____, and declare it is my Will, that I signed it willingly, that I executed it as my free and voluntary act for the purpose expressed herein, and that I am of legal age and sound mind.

_____

[Signature]

The foregoing instrument was on said date subscribed at the end thereof by _____, the above named testator who signed, published, and declared this instrument to be his/her Last Will and Testament in the presence of us and each of us, who thereupon at his/her request, in his/her presence, and in the presence of each other, have hereunto subscribed our names as witnesses thereto. We are of sound mind and proper age to witness a will and understand this to be his/her will, and to the best of our knowledge testator is of legal age to make a will, of sound mind, and under no constraint or undue influence.

_____ residing at _____
_____ residing at _____
_____ residing at _____

Initials: _____ _____ _____ _____   Page _____ of _____
        Testator   Witness   Witness   Witness

WILL
Unmarried with Adult Children

Will of _____

I, _____ of _____,
make this my Will. I revoke any other Wills and codicils made by me.

1. Family

I have _____ children, _____, my children.
The term "my children" includes the aforementioned children and all children born after the making of this will and all children adopted by me.

2. Residuary Estate

A. I give my residuary estate, that is, all of my property, real, personal, and mixed, of whatever kind and wherever situated, of which I may die possessed, in equal shares, to my children.

B. If a child does not survive me, then the deceased child's share devolves, in equal shares, to the deceased child's children. If none of the deceased child's children survive me, then this share devolves, in equal shares, to my surviving children.

C. If a deceased child's children are entitled to a share of my estate, I leave this bequest to my trustee to be held in trust under Article 4, "Grandchildren's Trust."

3. Appointment of Fiduciaries

A. Executor. I appoint _____ to serve as my executor. If _____ cannot serve, then I appoint _____ to serve as my executor.

B. Trustee. I appoint _____ to serve as my trustee. If _____ cannot serve, then I appoint _____ to serve as my trustee.

C. No bond shall be required of my executor or trustee.

4. Grandchild's Trust

My trustee shall hold the assets passing to my grandchildren in a separate trust for each grandchild under this article until that grandchild has reached the age of _____ years, the termination date.

A. Until the termination date, my trustee shall distribute to or for the benefit of my grandchild as much of the net income and principal as my trustee may consider appropriate for the grandchild's health, education, support, or maintenance, annually adding to principal any undistributed income.

B. Upon the termination date, my trustee shall distribute the remaining assets to the grandchild.

5. Miscellaneous

My executor and trustee shall exercise all powers conferred by law, in addition to the following powers, which are to be exercised in the best interest of my estate or trust.

A. To hold and retain any property owned by me.

B. To sell, exchange, or lease any property.

C. To vote stock; to convert securities belonging to my estate into other securities; and, to exercise all other rights and privileges of a person owning similar properties.

D. To settle claims.

E. To pay all debts and taxes.

F. To do all other acts necessary for the proper management, investment, and distribution of my estate or trust.

G. To take all actions to have the probate of this Will conducted as free of court supervision as possible.

I have signed this Will in the presence of the undersigned witnesses on this _____ day of _____, 20_____, at _____, State of _____, and declare it is my Will, that I signed it willingly, that I executed it as my free and voluntary act for the purpose expressed herein, and that I am of legal age and sound mind.

_____

[Signature]

The foregoing instrument was on said date subscribed at the end thereof by _____, the above named testator who signed, published, and declared this instrument to be his/her Last Will and Testament in the presence of us and each of us, who thereupon at his/her request, in his/her presence, and in the presence of each other, have hereunto subscribed our names as witnesses thereto. We are of sound mind and proper age to witness a will and understand this to be his/her will, and to the best of our knowledge testator is of legal age to make a will, of sound mind, and under no constraint or undue influence.

_____ residing at _____

_____ residing at _____

_____ residing at _____

WILL
Unmarried with Young Children

Will of _____

I, _____ of _____,
make this my Will. I revoke any other Wills and codicils made by me.

1. Family

I have _____ children, _____, my children.
The term "my children" includes the aforementioned children and all children born after the making of this will and all children adopted by me.

2. Residuary Estate

A. I give my residuary estate, that is, all of my property, real, personal, and mixed, of whatever kind and wherever situated, of which I may die possessed, to my children. If my youngest child has, on the date of my death, reached the age of _____ years, I leave this residuary estate outright, in equal shares, to my children. If my youngest child has not, on the date of my death, reached the age of _____ years, I leave this residuary estate to my trustee to be held in trust under Article 4, "Children's Trust."

B. If a child does not survive me and no "Children's Trust" is created according to Article 2.A above, then the deceased child's share devolves, in equal shares, to the deceased child's children. If none of the deceased child's children survive me, then this share devolves, in equal shares, to my surviving children.

C. If a deceased child's children are entitled to a share of my estate, I leave this bequest to my trustee to be held in trust under Article 5, "Grandchild's Trust."

3. Appointment of Fiduciaries

A. Executor. I appoint _____ to serve as my executor. If _____ cannot serve, then I appoint _____ to serve as my executor.

B. Guardian. If, at my death, any of my children are minors, and a guardian is needed for my minor children, I appoint _____to serve as my guardian. If _____ cannot serve, then I appoint _____ to serve as my guardian.

C. Trustee. I appoint _____ to serve as my trustee. If _____ cannot serve, then I appoint _____ to serve as my trustee.

D. No bond shall be required of my executor, trustee, or guardian.

4. Children's Trust

If a "Children's Trust" is created according to Article 2.A above, my trustee shall hold the assets passing to my children in trust under this article.

A. Until the termination date, my trustee shall distribute to or for the benefit of my children as much of the net income and principal as my trustee may consider appropriate for their health, education, support, or maintenance, annually adding to principal any undistributed income. My trustee may distribute income and principal unequally and may distribute to some children and not to others. My trustee may consider other income and assets readily available to my children in making distributions.

B. Upon the termination date, my trustee shall distribute the remaining assets, in equal shares, to my surviving children.

C. The termination date is the date on which my youngest living child has reached the age of _____ years.

5. Grandchild's Trust

My trustee shall hold the assets passing to my grandchildren in a separate trust for each grandchild under this article until that grandchild has reached the age of _____ years, the termination date.

A. Until the termination date, my trustee shall distribute to or for the benefit of my grandchild as much of the net income and principal as my trustee may consider appropriate for the grandchild's health, education, support, or maintenance, annually adding to principal any undistributed income.

B. Upon the termination date, my trustee shall distribute the remaining assets to the grandchild.

6. Miscellaneous

My executor and trustee shall exercise all powers conferred by law, in addition to the following powers, which are to be exercised in the best interest of my estate or trust.

A. To hold and retain any property owned by me.

B. To sell, exchange, or lease any property.

C. To vote stock; to convert securities belonging to my estate into other securities; and, to exercise all other rights and privileges of a person owning similar properties.

D. To settle claims.

E. To pay all debts and taxes.

F. To do all other acts necessary for the proper management, investment, and distribution of my estate or trust.

G. To take all actions to have the probate of this Will conducted as free of court supervision as possible.

I have signed this Will in the presence of the undersigned witnesses on this _____ day of _____, 20_____, at _____, State of _____, and declare it is my Will, that I signed it willingly, that I executed it as my free and voluntary act for the purpose expressed herein, and that I am of legal age and sound mind.

_____

[Signature]

The foregoing instrument was on said date subscribed at the end thereof by _____, the above named testator who signed, published, and declared this instrument to be his/her Last Will and Testament in the presence of us and each of us, who thereupon at his/her request, in his/her presence, and in the presence of each other, have hereunto subscribed our names as witnesses thereto. We are of sound mind and proper age to witness a will and understand this to be his/her will, and to the best of our knowledge testator is of legal age to make a will, of sound mind, and under no constraint or undue influence.

_____ residing at _____

_____ residing at _____

_____ residing at _____

Initials: _____ _____ _____ _____   Page _____ of _____

     Testator   Witness   Witness   Witness

This page intentionally blank.

WILL
Unmarried without Children

Will of _____

I, _____ of _____,
make this my Will. I revoke any other Wills and codicils made by me.

1. Residuary Estate

A. I give my residuary estate, that is, all of my property, real, personal, and mixed, of whatever kind and wherever situated, of which I may die possessed to:

1. _____
_____

2. _____
_____

3. _____
_____
_____
_____

2. Appointment of Fiduciaries

A. Executor. I appoint _____ to serve as my executor. If
_____ cannot serve, then I appoint _____
to serve as my executor.

B. Trustee. I appoint _____ to serve as my trustee. If
_____ cannot serve, then I appoint _____
to serve as my trustee.

C. No bond shall be required of my executor or trustee.

3. Young Person's Trust

My trustee shall hold the assets passing to young persons in a trust for each young person under this
article until that young person has reached the age of _____ years, the termination date.

A. Until the termination date, my trustee shall distribute to or for the benefit of the young
person as much of the net income and principal as my trustee may consider appropriate

for the young person's health, education, support, or maintenance, annually adding to principal any undistributed income.

B. Upon the termination date, my trustee shall distribute the remaining assets to the young person.

4. Miscellaneous

My executor shall exercise all powers conferred by law, in addition to the following powers, which are to be exercised in the best interest of my estate or trust.

A. To hold and retain any property owned by me.

B. To sell, exchange, or lease any property.

C. To vote stock; to convert securities belonging to my estate into other securities; and, to exercise all other rights and privileges of a person owning similar properties.

D. To settle claims.

E. To pay all debts and taxes.

F. To do all other acts necessary for the proper management, investment, and distribution of my estate or trust.

G. To take all actions to have the probate of this Will conducted as free of court supervision as possible.

I have signed this Will in the presence of the undersigned witnesses on this _____ day of _____, 20_____, at _____, State of _____, and declare it is my Will, that I signed it willingly, that I executed it as my free and voluntary act for the purpose expressed herein, and that I am of legal age and sound mind.

_____

[Signature]

The foregoing instrument was on said date subscribed at the end thereof by _____, the above named testator who signed, published, and declared this instrument to be his/her Last Will and Testament in the presence of us and each of us, who thereupon at his/her request, in his/her presence, and in the presence of each other, have hereunto subscribed our names as witnesses thereto. We are of sound mind and proper age to witness a will and understand this to be his/her will, and to the best of our knowledge testator is of legal age to make a will, of sound mind, and under no constraint or undue influence.

_____ residing at _____

_____ residing at _____

_____ residing at _____

Form A

Self-Proving Affidavit

(attach to Will)

STATE OF _____

COUNTY OF _____

We, _____, and _____, _____,
and _____, the testator and the witnesses, whose names are signed to the
attached or foregoing instrument in those capacities, personally appearing before the undersigned
authority and being first duly sworn, declare to the undersigned authority under penalty of perjury
that: 1) the testator declared, signed, and executed the instrument as his or her last Will; 2) he or she
signed it willingly, or directed another to sign for him or her; 3) he or she executed it as his or her
free and voluntary act for the purposes therein expressed; and 4) each of the witnesses, and the
request of the testator, in his or her hearing and presence and in the presence of each other, signed
the Will as witnesses, and that to the best of his or her knowledge the testator was at that time of full
legal age, of sound mind, and under no constraint or undue influence.

_____ (Testator)

_____ (Witness)

_____ (Witness)

_____ (Witness)

Subscribed, sworn, and acknowledged before me, _____, a notary public,
and by _____, the testator, and by _____,
_____ and _____, witnesses, this _____ day
of _____, 20_____.

_____

Notary Public

This page intentionally blank.

Form B

Self-Proving Affidavit
(attach to Will)

STATE OF _____

COUNTY OF _____

I, the undersigned, an officer authorized to administer oaths, certify that _____,
the testator, and _____, _____, and _____,
the witnesses, whose names are signed to the attached or foregoing instrument and whose signatures
appear below, having appeared before me and having been first been duly sworn, each then declared
to me that: 1) the attached or foregoing instrument is the last Will of the testator; 2) the testator willingly and voluntarily declared, signed, and executed the Will in the presence of the witnesses; 3) the
witnesses signed the Will upon the request of the testator, in the presence and hearing of the testator and in the presence of each other; 4) to the best knowledge of each witness, the testator was, at
the time of signing, of the age of majority (or otherwise legally competent to make a will), of sound
mind and memory, and under no constrain or undue influence; and, 5) each witness was and is
competent and of proper age to witness a Will.

_____ (Testator)

_____ (Witness)

_____ (Witness)

_____ (Witness)

Subscribed and sworn to before me by that _____, the testator, who is personally known to me or who has produced a _____ as identification, and by
_____, a witness, who is personally known to me or who has produced a
_____ as identification, and by _____, a witness, who is
personally known to me or who has produced a _____ as identification, and
by _____ a witness, who is personally known to me or who has produced a
_____ as identification, this this _____ day of _____,
20_____.

_____

Notary or other officer

This page intentionally blank.

Form C

Self-Proved Will Page—New Hampshire

(attach to Will)

STATE OF NEW HAMPSHIRE

COUNTY OF _____

The foregoing instrument was acknowledged before me this _____ [day], by _____, the testator; _____, _____, and _____, the witnesses, who under oath swear as follows:

1. The testator signed the instrument as his Will or expressly directed another to sign for him.

2. This was the testator's free and voluntary act for the purposes expressed in the Will.

3. Each witness signed at the request of the testator, in his presence, and in the presence of the other witness.

4. To the best of my knowledge, at the time of the signing the testator was at least 18 years of age, or if under 18 years was a married person, and was of sane mind and under no constraint or undue influence.

_____

Signature

_____

Official Capacity

This page intentionally blank.

Form D

Self-Proved Will Affidavit—Texas
(attach to Will)

STATE OF TEXAS

COUNTY OF _____

Before me, the undersigned authority, on this day personally appeared _____
_____, _____, and _____,
known to me to be the testator and the witnesses, respectively, whose names are subscribed to the
annexed or foregoing instrument in their respective capacities, and, all of said persons being by me
duly sworn, the said _____ testator, declared to me and
to the said witnesses in my presence that said instrument is his or her last Will and testament, and
that he or she had willingly made and executed it as his or her free act and deed, and the said witnesses, each on his or her oath stated to me in the presence and hearing of the said testator, that the
said testator had declared to them that said instrument is his or her last Will and testament, and that
he or she executed same as such and wanted each of them to sign it as a witness; and upon their oaths
each witness stated further that they did sign the same as witnesses in the presence of the said testator and at his or her request; that he or she was at the time eighteen years of age or over (or being
under such age, was or had been lawfully married, or was then a member of the armed forces of the
United States or an auxiliary thereof or of the Maritime Service) and was of sound mind; and that
each of said witnesses was then at least fourteen years of age.

_____ (Testator)

_____ (Witness)

_____ (Witness)

_____ (Witness)

Subscribed and sworn to before me by _____, the testator, and by
_____, _____ and _____
the witnesses, this _____ day of _____, 20_____.

Signed: _____

_____
Official Capacity of Officer

This page intentionally blank.

Health Care Advance Directive
Part I *Appointment of Health Care Agent*

1.   HEALTH CARE AGENT

I, _____ hereby appoint:
               PRINCIPAL

_____
               AGENT'S NAME

_____
               ADDRESS

_____
       HOME PHONE#   WORK PHONE#

as my agent to make health and personal care decisions for me as authorized in this document.

2.   ALTERNATE AGENTS

IF
- I revoke my Agent's authority; or
- my Agent becomes unwilling or unavailable to act; or
- if my agent is my spouse and I become legally separated or divorced,

I name the following (each to act alone and successively, in the order named) as alternates to my Agent:

A. First Alternate Agent _____

   Address_____

   Telephone_____

B. Second Alternate Agent_____

   Address _____

   Telephone _____

3. EFFECTIVE DATE AND DURABILITY

By this document I intend to create a health care advance directive. It is effective upon, and only during, any period in which I cannot make or communicate a choice regarding a particular health care decision. My agent, attending physician and any other necessary experts should determine that I am unable to make choices about health care.

4. AGENT'S POWERS

I give my Agent full authority to make health care decisions for me. My Agent shall follow my wishes as known to my Agent either through this document or through other means. When my agent interprets my wishes, I intend my Agent's authority to be as broad as possible, except for any limitations I state in this form. In making any decision, my Agent shall try to discuss the proposed decision with me to determine my desires if I am able to communicate in any way. If my Agent cannot determine the choice I would want, then my Agent shall make a choice for me based upon what my Agent believes to be in my best interests.

Unless specifically limited by Section 6, below, my Agent is authorized as follows:

A. To consent, refuse, or withdraw consent to any and all types of health care. Health care means any care, treatment, service or procedure to maintain, diagnose or otherwise affect an individual's physical or mental condition. It includes, but is not limited to, artificial respiration, nutritional support and hydration, medication and cardiopulmonary resuscitation;

B. To have access to medical records and information to the same extent that I am entitled, including the right to disclose the contents to others as appropriate for my health care;

C. To authorize my admission to or discharge (even against medical advice) from any hospital, nursing home, residential care, assisted living or similar facility or service;

D. To contract on my behalf for any health care related service or facility on my behalf, without my Agent incurring personal financial liability for such contracts;

E. To hire and fire medical, social service, and other support personnel responsible for my care;

F. To authorize, or refuse to authorize, any medication or procedure intended to relieve pain, even though such use may lead to physical damage, addiction, or hasten the moment of (but not intentionally cause) my death;

G. To make anatomical gifts of part or all of my body for medical purposes, authorize an autopsy, and direct the disposition of my remains, to the extent permitted by law;

H. To take any other action necessary to do what I authorize here, including (but not limited to) granting any waiver or release from liability required by any hospital, physician, or other health care provider; signing any documents relating to refusals of treatment or the leaving of a facility against medical advice; and pursuing any legal action in my name at the expense of my estate to force compliance with my wishes as determined by my Agent, or to seek actual or punitive damages for the failure to comply.

Health Care Advance Directive
Part II   *Instructions About Health Care*

5.   MY INSTRUCTIONS ABOUT END-OF-LIFE TREATMENT

(Initial only ONE of the following statements)

_____   **NO SPECIFIC INSTRUCTIONS.** My agent knows my values and wishes, so I do not wish to include any specific instructions here.

DIRECTIVE TO WITHHOLD OR WITHDRAW TREATMENT. Although I greatly value life, I also believe that at some point, life has such diminished value that medical treatment should be stopped, and I should be allowed to die. Therefore, I do not want to receive treatment, including nutrition and hydration, when the treatment will not give me a meaningful quality of life. I do not want my life prolonged...

_____   ... if the treatment will leave me in a condition of permanent unconsciousness, such as with an irreversible coma or a persistent vegetative state.

_____   ... if the treatment will leave me with no more than some consciousness and in an irreversible condition of complete, or nearly complete, loss of ability to think or communicate with others.

_____   ... if the treatment will leave me with no more than some ability to think or communicate with others, and the likely risks and burdens of treatment outweigh the expected benefits. Risks, burdens and benefits include consideration of length of life, quality of life, financial costs, and my personal dignity and privacy.

_____   **DIRECTIVE TO RECEIVE TREATMENT.** I want my life to be prolonged as long as possible, no matter what my quality of life.

_____   **DIRECTIVE ABOUT END-OF-LIFE TREATMENT IN MY OWN WORDS:**

_____

_____

_____

_____

_____

6. ANY OTHER HEALTH CARE INSTRUCTIONS OR LIMITATIONS OR MODIFICATIONS OF MY AGENTS POWERS

_____

_____

_____

_____

7. PROTECTION OF THIRD PARTIES WHO RELY ON MY AGENT

No person who relies in good faith upon any representations by my Agent or Alternate Agent(s) shall be liable to me, my estate, my heirs or assigns, for recognizing the Agent's authority.

8. DONATION OF ORGANS AT DEATH

Upon my death:
(Initial one)

_____ I do *not* wish to donate any organs or tissue, OR

_____ I give *any* needed organs, tissues, or parts, OR

_____ I give *only* the following organs, tissues, or parts:
(please specify)

_____

_____

My gift (if any) is for the following purposes:
(Cross out any of the following you do not want)

- ■ Transplant
- ■ Research
- ■ Therapy
- ■ Education

9.   NOMINATION OF GUARDIAN

If a guardian of my person should for any reason need to be appointed, I nominate my Agent (or his or her alternate then authorized to act), named above.

10.   ADMINISTRATIVE PROVISIONS

(All apply)

- ■ I revoke any prior health care advance directive.
- ■ This health care advance directive is intended to be valid in any jurisdiction in which it is presented.
- ■ A copy of this advance directive is intended to have the same effect as the original.

SIGNING THE DOCUMENT

BY SIGNING HERE I INDICATE THAT I UNDERSTAND THE CONTENTS OF THIS DOCUMENT AND THE EFFECT OF THIS GRANT OF POWERS TO MY AGENT.

I sign my name to this Health Care Advance Directive on this

_____ day of _____ , 20_____ .

My Signature_____

My Name_____

My current home address is_____

_____

_____

_____

174

WITNESS STATEMENT

I declare that the person who signed or acknowledged this document is personally known to me, that he/she signed or acknowledged this health care advance directive in my presence, and that he/she appears to be of sound mind and under no duress, fraud, or undue influence.

I am not:
- ■ the person appointed as agent by this document,
- ■ the principal's health care provider,
- ■ an employee of the principal's health care provider,
- ■ financially responsible for the principal's health care,
- ■ related to the principal by blood, marriage, or adoption, and,
- ■ to the best of my knowledge, a creditor of the principal/or entitled to any part of his/her estate under a will now existing or by operation of law.

Witness #1:

_____
Signature   Date

_____
Print Name

_____
Telephone

_____
Residence Address

Witness #2:

_____
Signature   Date

_____
Print Name

_____
Telephone

_____
Residence Address

NOTARIZATION

STATE OF _____)

COUNTY OF _____)

On this ____ day of _____, 20___,

the said _____, known to me (or satisfactorily proven) to be the person named in the foregoing instrument, personally appeared before me, a Notary Public, within and for the State and County aforesaid, and acknowledged that he or she freely and voluntarily executed the same for the purposes stated therein.

My Commission Expires:

_____
NOTARY PUBLIC

Power of Attorney

I _____ of _____, _____

appoint _____ of _____, _____

as my agent to act for me in any lawful way with respect to the following initialed subjects:

TO GRANT ALL OF THE FOLLOWING POWERS, INITIAL THE LINE IN FRONT OF (N) AND IGNORE THE LINES IN FRONT OF THE OTHER POWERS.

TO GRANT ONE OR MORE, BUT FEWER THAN ALL, OF THE FOLLOWING POWERS, INITIAL THE LINE IN FRONT OF EACH POWER YOU ARE GRANTING.

TO WITHHOLD A POWER, DO NOT INITIAL THE LINE IN FRONT OF IT. YOU MAY, BUT NEED NOT, CROSS OUT EACH POWER WITHHELD.

INITIAL

_____ (A)   Real property transactions.

_____ (B)   Tangible personal property transactions.

_____ (C)   Stock and bond transactions.

_____ (D)   Commodity and option transactions.

_____ (E)   Banking and other financial institution transactions.

_____ (F)   Business operating transactions.

_____ (G)   Insurance and annuity transactions.

_____ (H)   Estate, trust, and other beneficiary transactions.

_____ (I)   Claims and litigation.

_____ (J)   Personal and family maintenance.

_____ (K)   Benefits from Social Security, Medicare, Medicaid, or other governmental programs, or military service.

_____ (L)   Retirement plan transactions.

_____ (M)   Tax matters.

_____ (N)   ALL OF THE POWERS LISTED ABOVE. YOU NEED NOT INITIAL ANY OTHER LINES IF YOU INITIAL LINE (N).

ON THE FOLLOWING LINES YOU MAY GIVE SPECIAL INSTRUCTIONS LIMITING OR EXTENDING THE POWERS GRANTED TO YOUR AGENT.

_____

_____

_____

UNLESS YOU DIRECT OTHERWISE ABOVE, THIS POWER OF ATTORNEY IS EFFECTIVE IMMEDIATELY AND WILL CONTINUE UNTIL IT IS REVOKED.

This Power of Attorney will continue to be effective even though I become disabled, incapacitated, or incompetent.

I agree that any third party who receives a copy of this document may act under it. Revocation of the Power of Attorney is not effective as to a third party until the third party learns of the revocation. I agree to indemnify the third party for any claims that arise against the third party because of reliance on this Power of Attorney.

Signed this _____ day of _____, 20_____.

_____

[Signature]

_____

[Social Security Number]

WITNESSES:

_____   _____
Signature of Witness   Signature of Witness

_____   _____
Name   Name

_____   _____

_____   _____
Address   Address

State of _____)

County of _____)

This document was acknowledged before me on _____ by

_____, _____, _____,

[Name of Principal]   [Name of Witness]   [Name of Witness]

_____

[Signature of Notarial Officer]

[Seal, if any]

_____

[Title (and Rank)]

My commission expires: _____

BY ACCEPTING OR ACTING UNDER THE APPOINTMENT, THE AGENT ASSUMES THE FIDUCIARY AND OTHER LEGAL RESPONSIBILITIES OF AN AGENT.

CONSTRUCTION OF POWERS GENERALLY. By executing a statutory Power of Attorney, the principal, except as limited or extended by the principal in the Power of Attorney, empowers the agent, for that subject to:

(1) demand, receive, and obtain by litigation or otherwise, money or other thing of value to which the principal is, may become, or claims to be entitled; and conserve, invest, disburse, or use anything so received for the purposes intended;

(2) contract in any manner with any person, on terms agreeable to the agent, to accomplish a purpose of a transaction, and perform, rescind, reform, release, or modify the contract or another contract made by or on behalf of the principal;

(3) execute, acknowledge, seal, and deliver a deed, revocation, mortgage, lease, notice, check, release, or other instrument the agent considers desirable to accomplish a purpose of a transaction;

(4) prosecute, defend, submit to arbitration, settle, and propose or accept a compromise with respect to, a claim existing in favor of or against the principal or intervene in litigation relating to the claim;

(5) seek on the principal's behalf the assistance of a court to carry out an act authorized by the Power of Attorney;

(6) engage, compensate, and discharge an attorney, accountant, expert witness, or other assistant;

(7) keep appropriate records of each transaction, including an accounting of receipts and disbursements;

(8) prepare, execute, and file a record, report, or other document the agent considers desirable to safeguard or promote the principal's interest under a statute or governmental regulation;

(9) reimburse the agent for expenditures properly made by the agent in exercising the powers granted by the Power of Attorney; and

(10) in general, do any other lawful act with respect to the subject.

DEFINITIONS OF POWERS:

A. Real property transactions. The language granting power with respect to real property transactions empowers the agent to:

(1) accept as a gift or as security for a loan, reject, demand, buy, lease, receive, or otherwise acquire, an interest in real property or a right incident to real property;

(2) sell, exchange, convey with or without covenants, quitclaim, release, surrender, mortgage, encumber, partition, consent to partitioning, subdivide, apply for zoning, rezoning, or other governmental permits, plat or consent to platting, develop, grant options concerning, lease, sublease, or otherwise dispose of, an interest in real property or a right incident to real property;

(3) release, assign, satisfy, and enforce by litigation or otherwise, a mortgage, deed of trust, encumbrance, lien, or other claim to real property which exists or is asserted;

(4) do any act of management or of conservation with respect to an interest in real property, or a right incident to real property, owned, or claimed to be owned, by the principal, including:

    (i) insuring against a casualty, liability, or loss;

    (ii) obtaining or regaining possession, or protecting the interest or right, by litigation or otherwise;

    (iii) paying, compromising, or contesting taxes or assessments, or applying for and receiving refunds in connection with them; and

    (iv) purchasing supplies, hiring assistance or labor, and making repairs or alterations in the real property;

(5) use, develop, alter, replace, remove, erect, or install structures or other improvements upon real property in or incident to which the principal has, or claims to have, an interest or right;

(6) participate in a reorganization with respect to real property or a legal entity that owns an interest in or right incident to real property and receive and hold shares of stock or obligations received in a plan of reorganization, and act with respect to them, including:

    (i) selling or otherwise disposing of them;

    (ii) exercising or selling an option, conversion, or similar right with respect to them; and

    (iii) voting them in person or by proxy;

(7) change the form of title of an interest in or right incident to real property;

(8) dedicate to public use, with or without consideration, easements or other real property in which the principal has, or claims to have, an interest.

B. Tangible personal property transactions. The language granting power with respect to tangible personal property transactions empowers the agent to:

(1) accept as a gift or as security for a loan, reject, demand, buy, receive, or otherwise acquire ownership or possession of tangible personal property or an interest in tangible personal property;

(2) sell, exchange, convey with or without covenants, release, surrender, mortgage, encumber, pledge, hypothecate, create a security interest in, pawn, grant options concerning, lease, sublease to others, or otherwise dispose of tangible personal property or an interest in tangible personal property;

(3) release, assign, satisfy, or enforce by litigation or otherwise, a mortgage, security interest, encumbrance, lien, or other claim on behalf of the principal, with respect to tangible personal property or an interest in tangible personal property; and

(4) do an act of management or conservation with respect to tangible personal property or an interest in tangible personal property on behalf of the principal, including:

    (i) insuring against casualty, liability, or loss;

    (ii) obtaining or regaining possession, or protecting the property or interest, by litigation or otherwise;

    (iii) paying, compromising, or contesting taxes or assessments or applying for and receiving refunds in connection with taxes or assessments;

    (iv) moving from place to place;

    (v) storing for hire or on a gratuitous bailment; and

    (vi) using, altering, and making repairs or alterations.

C. Stock and bond transactions. The language granting power with respect to stock and bond transactions empowers the agent to buy, sell, and exchange stocks, bonds, mutual funds, and all other types of securities and financial instruments except commodity futures contracts and call and put options on stocks and stock indexes, receive certificates and other evidences of ownership with respect to securities, exercise voting rights with respect to securities in person or by proxy, enter into voting trusts, and consent to limitations on the right to vote.

D. Commodity and option transactions. The language granting power with respect to commodity and option transactions empowers the agent to buy, sell, exchange, assign, settle, and exercise commodity futures contracts and call and put options on stocks and stock indexes traded on a regulated option exchange, and establish, continue, modify, and terminate option accounts with a broker.

E: Banking and other financial institution transactions. The language granting power with respect to banking and other financial institution transactions empowers the agent to:

(1) continue, modify, and terminate an account or other banking arrangement made by or on behalf of the principal;

(2) establish, modify, and terminate an account or other banking arrangement with a bank, trust company, savings and loan association, credit union, thrift company, brokerage firm, or other financial institution selected by the agent;

(3) hire a safe deposit box or space in a vault;

(4) contract to procure other services available from a financial institution as the agent considers desirable;

(5) withdraw by check, order, or otherwise money or property of the principal deposited with or left in the custody of a financial institution;

(6) receive bank statements, vouchers, notices, and similar documents from a financial institution and act with respect to them;

(7) enter a safe deposit box or vault and withdraw or add to the contents;

(8) borrow money at an interest rate agreeable to the agent and pledge as security personal property of the principal necessary in order to borrow, pay, renew, or extend the time of payment of a debt of the principal;

(9) make, assign, draw, endorse, discount, guarantee, and negotiate promissory notes, checks, drafts, and other negotiable or nonnegotiable paper of the principal, or payable to the principal or the principal's order, receive the cash or other proceeds of those transactions, accept a draft drawn by a person upon the principal, and pay it when due;

(10) receive for the principal and act upon a sight draft, warehouse receipt, or other negotiable or nonnegotiable instrument;

(11) apply for and receive letters of credit, credit cards, and traveler's checks from a financial institution, and give an indemnity or other agreement in connection with letters of credit; and (12) consent to an extension of the time of payment with respect to commercial paper or a financial transaction with a financial institution.

F. Business operating transactions. The language granting power with respect to business operating transactions empowers the agent to:

(1) operate, buy, sell, enlarge, reduce, and terminate a business interest;

(2) to the extent that an agent is permitted by law to act for a principal and subject to the terms of the partnership agreement to:

    (i) perform a duty or discharge a liability and exercise a right, power, privilege, or option that the principal has, may have, or claims to have, under a partnership agreement, whether or not the principal is a partner;

    (ii) enforce the terms of a partnership agreement by litigation or otherwise; and

    (iii) defend, submit to arbitration, settle, or compromise litigation to which the principal is a party because of membership in the partnership;

(3) exercise in person or by proxy, or enforce by litigation or otherwise, a right, power, privilege, or option the principal has or claims to have as the holder of a bond, share, or other instrument of similar character and defend, submit to arbitration, settle, or compromise litigation to which the principal is a party because of a bond, share, or similar instrument;

(4) with respect to a business owned solely by the principal:

    (i) continue, modify, renegotiate, extend, and terminate a contract made with an individual or a legal entity, firm, association, or corporation by or on behalf of the principal with respect to the business before execution of the Power of Attorney;

    (ii) determine:

        (A) the location of its operation;

        (B) the nature and extent of its business;

        (C) the methods of manufacturing, selling, merchandising, financing, accounting, and advertising employed in its operation;

        (D) the amount and types of insurance carried;

        (E) the mode of engaging, compensating, and dealing with its accountants, attorneys, and other agents and employees;

    (iii) change the name or form of organization under which the business is operated and enter into a partnership agreement with other persons or organize a corporation to take over all or part of the operation of the business; and

    (iv) demand and receive money due or claimed by the principal or on the principal's behalf in the operation of the business, and control and disburse the money in the operation of the business;

(5) put additional capital into a business in which the principal has an interest;

(6) join in a plan of reorganization, consolidation, or merger of the business;

(7) sell or liquidate a business or part of it at the time and upon the terms the agent considers desirable;

(8) establish the value of a business under a buy-out agreement to which the principal is a party;

(9) prepare, sign, file, and deliver reports, compilations of information, returns, or other papers with respect to a business which are required by a governmental agency or instrumentality or which the agent considers desirable, and make related payments; and

(10) pay, compromise, or contest taxes or assessments and do any other act which the agent considers desirable to protect the principal from illegal or unnecessary taxation, fines, penalties, or assessments with respect to a business, including attempts to recover, in any manner permitted by law, money paid before or after the execution of the Power of Attorney.

G. Insurance and annuity transactions. The language granting power with respect to insurance and annuity transactions empowers the agent to:

(1) continue, pay the premium or assessment on, modify, rescind, release, or terminate a contract procured by or on behalf of the principal which insures or provides an annuity to either the principal or another person, whether or not the principal is a beneficiary under the contract;

(2) procure new, different, and additional contracts of insurance and annuities for the principal and the principal's spouse, children, and other dependents; and select the amount, type of insurance or annuity, and mode of payment;

(3) pay the premium or assessment on, modify, rescind, release, or terminate a contract of insurance or annuity procured by the agent;

(4) designate the beneficiary of the contract, but an agent may be named a beneficiary of the contract, or an extension, renewal, or substitute for it, only to the extent the agent was named as a beneficiary under a contract procured by the principal before executing the Power of Attorney;

(5) apply for and receive a loan on the security of the contract of insurance or annuity;

(6) surrender and receive the cash surrender value;

(7) exercise an election;

(8) change the manner of paying premiums;

(9) change or convert the type of insurance contract or annuity, with respect to which the principal has or claims to have a power described in this section;

(10) change the beneficiary of a contract of insurance or annuity, but the agent may not be designated a beneficiary except to the extent permitted by paragraph (4);

(11) apply for and procure government aid to guarantee or pay premiums of a contract of insurance on the life of the principal;

(12) collect, sell, assign, hypothecate, borrow upon, or pledge the interest of the principal in a contract of insurance or annuity; and

(13) pay from proceeds or otherwise, compromise or contest, and apply for refunds in connection with, a tax or assessment levied by a taxing authority with respect to a contract of insurance or annuity or its proceeds or liability accruing by reason of the tax or assessment.

H. Estate, trust, and other beneficiary transactions. The language granting power with respect to estate, trust, and other beneficiary transactions, empowers the agent to act for the principal in all matters that affect a trust, probate estate, guardianship, conservatorship, escrow, custodianship, or other fund from which the principal is, may become, or claims to be entitled, as a beneficiary, to a share or payment, including to:

(1) accept, reject, disclaim, receive, receipt for, sell, assign, release, pledge, exchange, or consent to a reduction in or modification of a share in or payment from the fund;

(2) demand or obtain by litigation or otherwise money or other thing of value to which the principal is, may become, or claims to be entitled by reason of the fund;

(3) initiate, participate in, and oppose litigation to ascertain the meaning, validity, or effect of a deed, will, declaration of trust, or other instrument or transaction affecting the interest of the principal;

(4) initiate, participate in, and oppose litigation to remove, substitute, or surcharge a fiduciary;

(5) conserve, invest, disburse, and use anything received for an authorized purpose; and

(6) transfer an interest of the principal in real property, stocks, bonds, accounts with financial institutions, insurance, and other property, to the trustee of a revocable trust created by the principal as settlor.

I. Claims and litigation. The language granting power with respect to claims and litigation empowers the agent to:

(1) assert and prosecute before a court or administrative agency a claim, a [claim for relief] [cause of action], counterclaim, offset, and defend against an individ-

ual, a legal entity, or government, including suits to recover property or other thing of value, to recover damages sustained by the principal, to eliminate or modify tax liability, or to seek an injunction, specific performance, or other relief;

(2) bring an action to determine adverse claims, intervene in litigation, and act as amicus curiae;

(3) in connection with litigation, procure an attachment, garnishment, libel, order of arrest, or other preliminary, provisional, or intermediate relief and use an available procedure to effect or satisfy a judgment, order, or decree;

(4) in connection with litigation, perform any lawful act, including acceptance of tender, offer of judgment, admission of facts, submission of a controversy on an agreed statement of facts, consent to examination before trial, and binding the principal in litigation;

(5) submit to arbitration, settle, and propose or accept a compromise with respect to a claim or litigation;

(6) waive the issuance and service of process upon the principal, accept service of process, appear for the principal, designate persons upon whom process directed to the principal may be served, execute and file or deliver stipulations on the principal's behalf, verify pleadings, seek appellate review, procure and give surety and indemnity bonds, contract and pay for the preparation and printing of records and briefs, receive and execute and file or deliver a consent, waiver, release, confession of judgment, satisfaction of judgment, notice, agreement, or other instrument in connection with the prosecution, settlement, or defense of a claim or litigation;

(7) act for the principal with respect to bankruptcy or insolvency proceedings, whether voluntary or involuntary, concerning the principal or some other person, with respect to a reorganization proceeding, or a receivership or application for the appointment of a receiver or trustee which affects an interest of the principal in property or other thing of value; and

(8) pay a judgment against the principal or a settlement made in connection with litigation and receive and conserve money, or other thing of value paid in settlement of or as proceeds of a claim or litigation.

J. Personal and family maintenance. The language granting power with respect to personal and family maintenance empowers the agent to:

(1) do the acts necessary to maintain the customary standard of living of the principal, the principal's spouse, children, and other individuals customarily or legally entitled to be supported by the principal, including providing living quarters by purchase, lease, or other contract, or paying the operating costs, including interest, amortization payments, repairs, and taxes on premises owned by the principal and occupied by those individuals;

(2) provide for the individuals described in paragraph (1) normal domestic help; usual vacations and travel expenses; and funds for shelter, clothing, food, appropriate education, and other current living costs;

(3) pay for the individuals described in paragraph (1) necessary medical, dental, and surgical care, hospitalization, and custodial care;

(4) continue any provision made by the principal, for the individuals described in paragraph (1), for automobiles or other means of transportation, including registering, licensing, insuring, and replacing them;

(5) maintain or open charge accounts for the convenience of the individuals described in paragraph (1) and open new accounts the agent considers desirable to accomplish a lawful purpose; and

(6) continue payments incidental to the membership or affiliation of the principal in a church, club, society, order, or other organization or to continue contributions to those organizations.

K. Benefits from social security, medicare, medicaid, or other governmental programs, or military service. The language granting power with respect to benefits from social security, medicare, Medicaid, or other governmental programs, or military service empowers the agent to:

(1) execute vouchers in the name of the principal for allowances and reimbursements payable by the United States or a foreign government or by a state or subdivision of a state to the principal, including allowances and reimbursements for transportation of the individuals described in Section 13(1), and for shipment of their household effects;

(2) take possession and order the removal and shipment of property of the principal from a post, warehouse, depot, dock, or other place of storage or safekeeping, either governmental or private, and execute and deliver a release, voucher, receipt, bill of lading, shipping ticket, certificate, or other instrument for that purpose;

(3) prepare, file, and prosecute a claim of the principal to a benefit or assistance, financial or otherwise, to which the principal claims to be entitled, under a statute or governmental regulation;

(4) prosecute, defend, submit to arbitration, settle, and propose or accept a compromise with respect to any benefits the principal may be entitled to receive; and

(5) receive the financial proceeds of a claim of the type described in this section, conserve, invest, disburse, or use anything received for a lawful purpose.

L. Retirement plan transactions. The language granting power with respect to retirement plan transactions empowers the agent to:

(1) select payment options under any retirement plan in which the principal participates, including plans for self-employed individuals;

(2) designate beneficiaries under those plans and change existing designations;

(3) make voluntary contributions to those plans;

(4) exercise the investment powers available under any self-directed retirement plan;

(5) make "rollovers" of plan benefits into other retirement plans;

(6) if authorized by the plan, borrow from, sell assets to, and purchase assets from the plan; and

(7) waive the right of the principal to be a beneficiary of a joint or survivor annuity if the principal is a spouse who is not employed.

M. Tax matters. The language granting power with respect to tax matters empowers the agent to:

(1) prepare, sign, and file federal, state, local, and foreign income, gift, payroll, Federal Insurance Contributions Act returns, and other tax returns, claims for refunds, requests for extension of time, petitions regarding tax matters, and any other tax-related documents, including receipts, offers, waivers, consents (including consents and agreements under Internal Revenue Code Section 2032A or any successor section), closing agreements, and any power of attorney required by the Internal Revenue Service or other taxing authority with respect to a tax year upon which the statute of limitations has not run and the following 25 tax years;

(2) pay taxes due, collect refunds, post bonds, receive confidential information, and contest deficiencies determined by the Internal Revenue Service or other taxing authority;

(3) exercise any election available to the principal under federal, state, local, or foreign tax law; and

(4) act for the principal in all tax matters for all periods before the Internal Revenue Service, and any other taxing authority.

Form derived from Uniform Statutory Form Power of Attorney Act, NCCUSL©1989, with permission.

Index

D

E

M

N

W

Y

About the Author

Joy S. Chambers has practiced law for nearly three decades in Metropolitan Washington, D.C. For the past twenty-five years, she has had a successful private practice in historic Old Town Alexandria, VA, specializing in wills, trusts, and estates. Her interest in this field has expanded to include a broad spectrum of social issues facing older Americans. Ms. Chambers, who is trained in psychiatry as well as law, is particularly interested in how the mind ages, and specializes in assisting clients in planning for potential disabilities by using available legal tools.

Ms. Chambers is committed to educating the public about the issues she sees in her daily practice, seeing her advocacy and outreach as a logical extension of her practice. She produces and hosts a weekly cable television program, "Maturity," which explores issues of interest to seniors. Her column, "Maturity Watch," appears regularly in the Alexandria Gazette. She is a frequent contributor to other publications with senior audiences, including the AARP Bulletin and McGraw-Hill's Elder Care/Law, and has appeared on CNN and MSNBC.

Since establishing her practice, Ms. Chambers has been an enthusiastic educator of law students at local universities. As Adjunct Professor at the George Washington University Law School, she has designed and taught an innovative course, Law and Psychiatry, which utilized films concerned with mental illness as a springboard for discussions. Recently, Ms. Chambers extended her academic activities into the international arena, teaching a two-week course in American inheritance and disability planning law at the National University Law School in Bangalore, India—thus offering members of another culture the opportunity to learn aspects of this country's legal system. She has been invited to teach similar courses at other Indian universities in late 2005 and early 2006.

Ms. Chambers has advanced elder concerns in a variety of civic capacities. She was appointed by the governor of Virginia to the Joint Legislative Subcommittee on Legal Guardianship, and frequently advises state legislators on probate and related concerns. A member of the Virginia and District of Columbia Bar Associations, she has served on various committees making recommendations about legal issues. She has served on the Executive Committee of the Alexandria Commission of Aging and is a former Vice President of the Northern Virginia Estate Planning Council.

Ms. Chambers earned her JD degree at the George Washington University Law School, with additional studies at the University of London prior to practicing law. She has been a visiting researcher at Harvard Law and Medical Schools, and is currently pursuing studies in Islamic law and international relations at the Johns Hopkins School of International Affairs. Most recently, Ms. Chambers has been named a Senior Specialist for the Fulbright Program.

Ms. Chambers is a native of Mobile, Alabama.